P

MW01063428

The Dead Celebrity Cookbook . . .

"God, is it brilliant!"

—**Ted Allen,** *Chopped*

"These are the stars I grew up watching and they deserve to be remembered even if they were more talented on screen than they were in the kitchen."

—**Rosie O'Donnell**

"One of our ten favorite pop culture cookbooks . . . most enticing . . ."

—**Flavorwire,** *Huffington Post*

"Dead tasty!"

—*Marie Claire*

"While Halloween might come only once a year, there's never a bad time for *The Dead Celebrity Cookbook*."

—*bonappetit.com*

"Flip on a movie channel and get cooking! Required reading."

—**Billy Heller,** *New York Post*

"A veritable who's who of Hollywood's Golden Age."

—**Sara Bonisteel,** epicurious.com

"Celebrities like Elizabeth Taylor and Andy Warhol may be gone, but their favorite dishes will never be forgotten. Try one tonight!"

—**oprah.com**

THE DEAD CELEBRITY COOKBOOK

presents

CHRISTMAS in TINSELTOWN

Celebrity Recipes and Hollywood Memories from Six Feet Under the Mistletoe

FRANK DECARO

Health Communications, Inc.
Deerfield Beach, Florida

www.hcibooks.com

Library of Congress Cataloging-in-Publication information
is available through the Library of Congress.

ISBN-13: 978-0-7573-1700-2 (paperback)
ISBN-10: 0-7573-1700-6 (paperback
ISBN-13: 978-0-7573-1701-9 (e-book)
ISBN-10: 0-7573-1701-4 (e-book)

Publisher: Health Communications, Inc.
      3201 S.W. 15th Street
      Deerfield Beach, FL 33442–8190

Cover image ©GettyImages.com
Cover design and interior illustrations by Larissa Hise Henoch
Interior design and formatting by Lawna Patterson Oldfield

TO JIM,
WHO DOES
CHRISTMAS BETTER
THAN ANYONE

contents

INTRODUCTION

N O ONE MAKES A BIGGER DEAL out of holidays than we do at our house and no ticket—not even for *Book of Mormon*—is harder to secure than a seat at our Christmas Eve table. We don't care about religious beliefs; we just insist our guests be totally enthusiastic. We demand they commit themselves 110 percent to the celebration. Like a certain reality competition, we *have* voted friends off Christmas Island. It's rough at our place on December 24, but it's worth it.

Every year brings a new theme to our festivity. We choose them as much as five years in advance and start collecting ornaments, glassware, china, tabletop decorations, linens, and anything that fits the motif we're going for. If the producers of *Hoarders* ever want to do a Christmas special, I'm their man.

So far we've done a hot pink and chartreuse color scheme (what I called "*Laugh-In* Christmas"), a candy theme we referred to as "Operation: Gum-drop," and an all-Hawaiian holiday dubbed "Mele Kaliki-Tiki." We did a TV-and-movie-star-obsessed "Pop Culture" celebration one year, a royally resplendent "Purple-and-Gold" motif another, a sophisticated "Black-and-White" look, a Chanukah-inclusive "Blue and Silver" design, and "Bells, Bells, Bells," which was just what it sounds like. This year, it's going to be

"Merry and Bright." Next year, it's "Felt." The year after that is "Peppermint Twisted." I'm thinking stripes.

I told you, we plan ahead.

So when it came time to do a new volume of *The Dead Celebrity Cookbook*—a book that became something of an international sensation—it seemed only natural to create a holiday edition. After all, Christmas may be the most wonderful time of the year, but it can leave a host or hostess wondering what to serve that he or she has never served before.

Thanks to the book you're holding, you can create a holiday celebration that's retro but completely new: Christmas the way they did it in Hollywood back when the phrase "celebrity chef" meant a singer or actor who was also handy in the kitchen, not some hotsy-totsy cook with a cable show.

This year, whip up Peggy Lee's Holiday Halibut Casserole on Christmas Eve, an especially appropriate dish if you traditionally don't eat meat that night. On Christmas Day, make Joan Blondell's Buffet Ham, and then use the leftovers in Nat "King" Cole's Baked Ham Loaf to feed all your return-happy mall-crawlers on the 26th. Instead of just watching *Miracle on 34th Street* this year, cook up a batch of Natalie Wood's Beef Stroganoff to savor while you view. If you're more of a *Pee-wee's Playhouse Christmas Special* type, there's Dinah Shore's Fruitcake. The best thing about these easy recipes is that you can make them without roasting your chestnuts on an open fire. There's no stress here.

With *Christmas in Tinseltown*, you can put the kitsch back in your kitchen and lend that tired holiday ham some much-needed glam. In the pages that follow are more than 60 recipes for appetizers, main dishes, sides, and desserts from such beloved stars as Bing Crosby, Burl Ives, Bea Arthur, and the Grinch himself, Boris Karloff. All are linked to Christmas in some special way. For years, I've been collecting stars' recipes via out-of-print cookbooks and musty biographies that I picked up at flea markets, old appliance manuals, tattered giveaway pamphlets and vintage magazines that I found on eBay, newspaper clippings forwarded to me by listeners of my Sirius XM radio show, and more.

In this book's themed chapters—"It's a Wonderful Lunch," "Eat Meat in St. Louis," and "Munch of the Wooden Soldiers," to name a few—you'll find a variety of recipes, such as James Stewart's Barbecued Ribs, Vincente Minnelli's Chicken, Oliver Hardy's Baked Apples, Jimmy Durante's German Cole Slaw, Barbara Stanwyck's Kipfels, and a Christmas Cup worthy of Santa himself from Edmund Gwenn. None appeared in *The Dead Celebrity Cookbook*, by the way—all are exclusive to this volume. These celebrities may be six feet under the mistletoe, but their culinary prowess lives on.

I hope you'll think of this book as your guide to the best food, music, movies, and TV shows that the holidays have ever had to offer. I say "holidays" because there's a New Year's Eve chapter in *Christmas in Tinseltown* as well. It didn't seem right to do a book that celebrated stars gone by without including Dick Clark and Guy Lombardo. For decades, they made our holidays bubblier. My wish is that the recipes and the viewing and listening suggestions contained in *Christmas in Tinseltown* will do the same for you for many years to come.

1

IT'S a WONDERFUL LUNCH

When I was a kid growing up in the '70s, *It's a Wonderful Life* wasn't so much a Christmas movie as a Christmas-is-coming movie. My grandmother would always check off the program listing in *TV Guide* in red pencil to make sure we'd remember to tune in. Watching that movie was like seeing Santa Claus sleigh his way down Broadway at the end of the Macy's Thanksgiving Day Parade. It meant that pretty soon we'd all be shouting "Merry Christmas!" as vociferously as George Bailey (James Stewart) does at the film's culmination.

I never fully appreciated *It's a Wonderful Life* as a child. In those days, my favorite part of Frank Capra's 1946 holiday film classic was the temporarily wingless angel named Clarence, played by Henry Travers. But as Karen Walker always said on *Will & Grace*, "Kids are dumb." Now he just bugs me. As George complains at his lowest ebb in the movie, "You look about like the kind of angel I'd get." Clarence is basically a doofus in a nightshirt; no wonder it takes him so long to earn his wings. And as for those chitchatting stars in the heavens, who thought *that* was a good idea? Sorry Mr. Capra, but that's just K-O-R-N!

In fact, much of *It's a Wonderful Life* is corny, even the title. In our cynical age, you'd think we'd dismiss the movie as just so much holiday goo. But we don't. The performances in it are just too good to resist. There's Stewart as the savings-and-loan officer George—caring but complex, pleasant but plagued by darkness—and Donna Reed as his wife Mary Hatch Bailey, gorgeous and romantic and funny and strong. And then there's Lionel Barrymore, with vinegar in his veins, as Henry Potter, "the richest and meanest man in the county." Who would stoop so low as to steal $8,000 from dizzy Uncle Billy (Thomas Mitchell) at Christmas? Even Scrooge would call that bum an ice-hole.

The film has so many memorable scenes: the shovel-riding accident when

Stewart, Reed, and their *Wonderful* kids.

George saves his brother, the poison prescription at the pharmacy, the school dance when everyone ends up in the drink, the run on the bank that costs George and Mary their honeymoon, the couple's make-do romantic dinner in the ramshackle house that would become their family home, George's breakdown before his justifiably terrified kids, his visions of the world had he never been born, and especially, his climactic moment as he runs through the streets of Bedford Falls shouting at the top of his lungs, so very happy to be alive on Christmas. The moment that gets me is when George tells Mary in a whisper that comes from his heart via his loins, "You're wonderful!" I could plotz.

As film critic Roger Ebert once wrote, "What's remarkable about *It's a Wonderful Life* is how well it holds up over the years. It's one of those time-less movies like *Casablanca* or *The Third Man* that improves with age."

Here's the weird thing, though. When *It's a Wonderful Life* premiered in theatres in limited release at the end of 1946, it wasn't much of a hit. Reviews were mixed. The *New York Times,* for instance, said the film was undone by its own sentimentality. The FBI branded it a commie undertaking because it vilified bankers. The movie didn't even make the top 25 grossing pictures of 1947, the year it went into wide release. Yes, it was nominated for five Academy Awards, but it won none. Most of the trophies went to *The Best Years of Our Lives.*

It's a Wonderful Life achieved the status of a holiday classic only after it was broadcast on television—again and again—in the 1970s and '80s. Since then, it truly has become part of pop culture as families began making an annual viewing of the film a holiday ritual. No one was more surprised at the film's rise to the top decades after its release than the man who made the movie himself. "It's the damnedest thing I've ever seen," Frank Capra told the *Wall Street Journal* in the early 1980s. "The film has a life of its own now."

Much to the director's dismay, a gender-reversed TV movie version called *It Happened One Christmas* starring Marlo Thomas was made in 1977. Capra called it "plagiarism," but ratings were good. In more recent years, the film has been toyed with on shows from *The Simpsons* to *Raising Hope*, and it was remade again in the 1990s as *Clarence*. Every December, Seneca Falls, a town in the Finger Lakes region of upstate New York that considers itself the real-life model for the fictional Bedford Falls, celebrates the film. There's even an *It's a Wonderful Life* museum there.

My favorite tribute to *It's a Wonderful Life* remains the 1986 *Saturday Night Live* spoof that claimed to be the "lost ending" of the film. In the black-and-white clip, available on the Internet, George (Dana Carvey), Mary (Jan Hooks), and George's brother Harry (Dennis Miller) beat the living Christmas out of Henry Potter (Jon Lovitz) while the town sings "Auld Lang Syne." It's an ending out of *Suddenly Last Summer*, but it's very satisfying.

You can satisfy your taste for blood in a much more civil way by cooking up James Stewart's Spare Ribs with Barbecue Sauce. Add a side of Lionel Barrymore's Fettuccine Alfredo and make Donna Reed's Lemon Bundt Cake and you've got dinner. As for Beulah Bondi's Baked Eggs? Make that dish on Christmas morning.

It's a wonderful lunch.

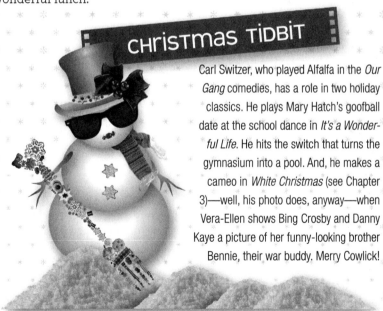

CHRISTMAS TIDBIT

Carl Switzer, who played Alfalfa in the *Our Gang* comedies, has a role in two holiday classics. He plays Mary Hatch's goofball date at the school dance in *It's a Wonderful Life*. He hits the switch that turns the gymnasium into a pool. And, he makes a cameo in *White Christmas* (see Chapter 3)—well, his photo does, anyway—when Vera-Ellen shows Bing Crosby and Danny Kaye a picture of her funny-looking brother Bennie, their war buddy. Merry Cowlick!

THE ALLITERATIVELY APPEALING Beulah Bondi carved out a niche in Hollywood as a highly respected character actress in a long career that ran from the classic 1932 sizzler *Rain* with Joan Crawford to a couple of episodes of *The Waltons* in the 1970s, a guest role that earned her an Emmy Award.

She played James Stewart's mother not only in *It's a Wonderful Life*, but also in 1939's *Mr. Smith Goes to Washington* and two other films. Her greatest performance, some say, was in the 1937 melodrama *Make Way for Tomorrow* for Leo McCarey, who, twenty years later, directed *An Affair to Remember*.

Bondi made her stage debut at age seven in her native Valparaiso, Indiana. But it took her until her thirties to make it to Broadway, and Hollywood didn't come calling until she was past forty.

In her movie debut, 1931's *Street Scene*, Bondi re-created the role that had brought her acclaim on Broadway. She went on to appear in the 1936 drama *The Trail of the Lonesome Pine*, the 1938 Cecil B. DeMille swashbuckler *The Buccaneer*, the 1941 Cary Grant romance *Penny Serenade*, and the lurid 1948 insane-asylum drama *The Snake Pit*. J'adore that last one.

From the '50s onward, Bondi alternated between film and television, performing in a couple of *Tammy* movies, and turning up on such series as *Alfred Hitchcock Presents, Wagon Train, Route 66, Perry Mason*, and on her frequent co-star's ill-fated early 1970s sitcom, *The Jimmy Stewart Show*. Yet again, she played Stewart's mother. Although Bondi made playing mothers— and later grandmothers—her specialty, she never married nor had kids in real life. Instead, she left behind fabulous performances and a recipe for a wonderful brunch dish.

Beulah Bondi's Baked Eggs

Shell and cut the hard-boiled eggs in half lengthwise. Place them cut-side-up in a greased baking dish. Sprinkle the eggs with salt and pepper. Now make a white sauce. Start by making a roux: Over low heat, melt the butter and stir in the flour. Then add the salt, cream, and milk. Once the mixture begins to thicken, add the sour cream and heat through. Pour the white sauce over the eggs. Sprinkle with nutmeg and top with the parmesan cheese. Bake at 350 degrees for 30 minutes or until bubbly.

8 hard-boiled eggs

Salt and pepper, to taste

2 tablespoons butter

2 tablespoons flour

½ teaspoon salt

½ cup cream

½ cup milk

1 pint sour cream

Nutmeg, to taste

1 cup Parmesan cheese

*Y*OU CAN'T TAKE IT WITH YOU, Mr. Smith Goes to Washington, The Philadelphia Story, Rope, It's a Wonderful Life, Harvey, Rear Window, The Man Who Knew Too Much, Vertigo, Bell Book and Candle, Anatomy of a Murder, The Man Who Shot Liberty Valance, and that's only counting up to 1962.

It's no stretch to say that James "Jimmy" Stewart, a man whose signature stammer made him fodder for generations of impressionists, starred in more classic films than anyone.

Consider this: Stewart is on more of the American Film Institute's top ten lists than any other leading actor. He beat out every other actor with more entries on *Entertainment Weekly*'s ranking of the 100 Greatest Films of All Time, too. At least ten of his films are in the National Film Registry. He was nominated for five Academy Awards, winning one for *The Philadelphia Story* in 1941 and receiving a lifetime achievement award in 1985. Is it any wonder that *It's a Wonderful Life* director Frank Capra called him "probably the best actor who's ever hit the screen"? Hell, even Joan Crawford said nice things about him!

An athlete and an accomplished accordion player, Stewart made his way to acting while studying architecture at Princeton. After cutting his teeth in summer stock productions on Cape Cod in the early 1930s, he made his Broadway debut. The part had only a few lines but *The New Yorker* noted that he always got a round of spontaneous applause when he left the stage. In 1935, encouraged by his friend (and former New York roommate) Henry Fonda, Stewart signed with MGM. His first juicy film part came the following year in *After the Thin Man*.

Once Stewart began collaborating with Capra in 1938 for *You Can't Take It with You*, there was no stopping him. Over the years, he worked with—and became a favorite of—such powerhouse directors as George Cukor, Cecil B. DeMille, Ernst Lubitsch, George Stevens, Billy Wilder, Don Siegel, John Ford, and, of course, Alfred Hitchcock. You haven't lived until you've seen Stewart in *Vertigo*. And, with good looks and perennially boyish charm, he had no trouble attracting beautiful women. Stewart dated Ginger Rogers, was pals with Margaret Sullavan with whom he starred in 1940's *The Shop Around the Corner*, and had a mad affair with Norma Shearer before settling down with Gloria, his wife of 45 years.

Stewart's later work—a couple of short-lived TV series and such films as *Airport '77*, *The Big Sleep*, and *The Magic of Lassie* in the '70s—weren't up to his earlier stuff, but audiences never grew tired of seeing him. He continued working into the 1990s. He explained his popularity like this: "I suppose people can relate to being me while they *dream* about being John Wayne." Sorry, pilgrim, but many of us will take Stewart over Wayne any day.

Here's an appropriate recipe, pardner.

James Stewart's Spareribs with Barbecue Sauce

Preheat the oven to 350 degrees. Cut the spareribs into two-rib pieces. Place the spareribs on a rimmed cookie sheet and season with salt and pepper. Place a lemon slice on each piece and then sprinkle each with some chopped onion. Set aside, covered.

Now prepare the barbecue sauce. Sauté the yellow onion and the garlic in the butter, cooking them until soft but not brown. Add the remaining ingredients and simmer for 30 minutes, stirring frequently.

Put the spareribs into the preheated oven and bake for 45 minutes, basting them with the barbecue sauce every once in a while, and turning them several times so they cook evenly.

Serve the remaining barbecue sauce on the side.

Spareribs

10 pounds spareribs

Salt and pepper, to taste

2 lemons, thinly sliced

1 large onion, chopped

Barbecue Sauce

1 yellow onion, grated

1 clove garlic, minced

2 tablespoons butter

1 teaspoon salt

1 teaspoon chili powder

½ teaspoon celery seed

½ cup brown sugar

½ cup vinegar

1 cup chili sauce

1 cup ketchup

2 cups water

Tabasco sauce, to taste

Lionel Barrymore, 1878–1954

H E WAS A MEMBER OF SHOW BUSINESS'S most illustrious family—one that continues to be known today via his great-niece Drew—and he won the Academy Award for his powerful performance as an alcoholic defense attorney in the 1931 pre-Code drama *A Free Soul*, starring Norma Shearer, Leslie Howard, and Clark Gable. But no matter what Lionel Barrymore did as an actor, director, composer, or author, he will always be known, first and foremost, as the Scrooge-like villain Henry Potter of *It's a Wonderful Life*.

Barrymore began acting on stage before the turn of the twentieth century, and while in his twenties appeared on Broadway. He made his screen debut in 1911—some claim it was even earlier—and went on to make at least 75 shorts in the next three years. He worked with D. W. Griffith and other silent film legends such as Mary Pickford and Lillian Gish. Later he moved on to features, sometimes acting in a half dozen of them a year. With his theatrically trained voice, the advent of talkies proved no obstacle for him.

Among Barrymore's best-known pictures are 1928's *Sadie Thompson* with Gloria Swanson, 1937's *Captains Courageous* starring Academy Award-winner Spencer Tracy, the 1938 Frank Capra comedy *You Can't Take It with You*, the classic 1946 western *Duel in the Sun*, and 1948's *Key Largo*, the final picture to pair Humphrey Bogart and Lauren Bacall. Barrymore did a string of *Dr. Kildare* pictures in the '30s and '40s, too, and he had a role in the 1944 weepie *Since You Went Away*, starring Claudette Colbert. It's a great film.

Audiences always adored seeing more than one Barrymore in a picture. Lionel appeared with his brother John in 1932's *Grand Hotel*, 1933's *Dinner at Eight,* and in a couple of other movies. He, John, and their sister Ethel appeared together in only one film, 1932's *Rasputin and the Empress.* After John's death, Ethel and Lionel appeared together in Lionel's last film, playing themselves in 1953's *Main Street to Broadway.* Are you getting all this down?

Somehow, he found time to cook. This simple recipe is credited to him.

CHRISTMAS TIDBIT

Don't you love it when a star of one holiday classic bitches about a star of another? After appearing in the 1943 mystery *Dr. Gillespie's Criminal Case* with child actress Margaret O'Brien, who'd go on to play Tootie in *Meet Me in St. Louis*, Lionel Barrymore said, "If that child had been born in the Middle Ages, she'd have been burned as a witch." When you read Chapter 5 and watch the 1944 Judy Garland musical, you'll understand why.

Lionel Barrymore's Fettuccine Alfredo

Boil fettuccine in salted water according to package directions. Drain. In large serving bowl, toss hot pasta with butter until melted. Sprinkle with cheese and gently toss again to combine. Serve immediately.

1½ pounds fettuccine noodles

Salt

½ pound butter, at room temperature, cut into cubes

1½ cups grated Parmesan cheese

BEFORE SHE WAS THE SUBURBAN HOUSEWIFE to end all suburban housewives in *The Donna Reed Show* from 1958 to 1966—only Barbara Billingsley of *Leave It to Beaver* ever came close—Donna Reed won an Oscar for playing a prostitute in the 1953 World War II classic *From Here to Eternity*. Talk about range!

But every year, when *It's a Wonderful Life* comes on, Reed is Mary Hatch Bailey and all her other roles fade away, at least temporarily. As the wife of the despondent George (James Stewart), Reed is "remarkably poised and gracious," to use the words of *New York Times* reviewer Bosley Crowther, who rarely seemed to like anything. Roger Ebert, a big fan of the film, says her chemistry with Stewart is "wonderfully romantically charged."

It seems strange then that Reed had no intentions of being a professional actress. She was going to be a teacher. But she was spotted doing stage work in Los Angeles, and eventually signed with MGM in 1941, making her film debut in a gangster picture called *The Get-Away*. That first year, she appeared in *Shadow of the Thin Man*, too, and the following year, *The Courtship of Andy Hardy*.

Among her other early films were 1943's *The Human Comedy* written by William Saroyan; and, in 1945, *The Picture of Dorian Gray* starring George Sanders, and *They Were Expendable* with John Wayne. After *It's a Wonderful Life*, Reed made 1947's *Green Dolphin Street*, the 1952 film-noir *Scandal Sheet*, and the 1956 biopic *The Benny Goodman Story* with Steve Allen. Her eponymous TV show, now out on DVD, gave her immortality.

Late in her life, Reed returned to television, replacing Barbara Bel Geddes as Miss Ellie on *Dallas* for the 1984–85 season. But when the original actress decided to return, Reed was shown the door. She sued for breach of contract and reportedly settled for more than a million dollars. A biography of Reed quotes her as saying, "Nobody ever said showbiz was easy, fair, fun, or filled with nice people. *Dallas* is the pits." Still, in 2006, Reed was nominated for a—get this!—Most Irreplaceable Replacement trophy at the TV Land Awards. She didn't win, but she was long dead by then, anyway. Her Lemon Bundt Cake lives on, though.

CHRISTMAS TIDBIT

In "A Very Merry Christmas," a 1958 episode of *The Donna Reed Show*, nobody wants Donna Stone's fruitcake as a Christmas tip. The postman, drycleaner, and paperboy all would rather have cash. But she finds the real holiday spirit in the heart of a janitor (played by silent movie great Buster Keaton) who dresses up as Santa and cheers up the children's ward at the hospital where her sexy husband, Dr. Alex Stone (Carl Betz), works. The installment is available on the series' Season One box set and on a holiday compilation DVD called "Merry Sitcom! Christmas Classics from TV's Golden Age." It's primo *Donna*.

DONNA REED'S
LEMON BUNDT CAKE

Preheat the oven to 325 degrees. Mix all of the ingredients in the bowl of an electric mixer at low speed until combined. Then beat for 4 minutes at high speed. Pour the batter into a greased and floured Bundt pan. Bake for 50 minutes. Cool in the pan 10 minutes, then invert onto a rack to cool completely. Glaze with pourable icing or sprinkle with powdered sugar before serving.

1 (18.25 ounce) lemon cake mix

1 (3.4 ounce) box instant lemon pudding

½ cup vegetable oil

4 eggs

1 cup water

2

MiRACLE WHiP ON 34TH STREET

Maybe the bearded little fellow who calls himself Kris Kringle is a total whack job, promising harried shoppers that the floors around their Christmas trees will be cluttered with all the right presents on December 25. But what if the crazy old coot really is Santa Claus? For more than sixty-five years, holiday audiences have been asking themselves that question every Christmas and coming to believe, as little Susan Walker does, that the special Mr. K really is the genuine North Pole article.

By the end of *Miracle on 34th Street*—the original, not the 1994 why-did-they-bother? remake with Richard Attenborough—you really do think the man is who he says he is. Since its premiere in May (go figure) 1947, the film has become the best-loved holiday movie of all time. Face it: Christmas just isn't Christmas until you've watched Natalie Wood tug Edmund Gwenn's beard at least once.

As great as the film turned out, it almost didn't get made.

Legendary Hollywood producer Darryl F. Zanuck thought *Miracle* was just too saccharine to succeed. But writer-director George Seaton—and star John Payne—convinced him otherwise and the rest is Christmas history.

Maureen O'Hara, best known at the time for her role in *How Green Was My Valley*, stars as Doris Walker, a department store event planner who is divorced (a controversial plot point at the time) and has one very smart child (Wood). The dashing John Payne, who made four films with O'Hara over the years, plays Fred Gailey, the attorney who falls for her and makes sure that the man with the bag doesn't get stuck holding it. He proves that Kringle (Gwenn) is the one and only Santa Claus with a little help from the post office. Jack Albertson—yes, *that* Jack Albertson, the one from *Chico and the Man*—plays a mail sorter.

Tugs Not Hugs: Gwenn, Wood, and Payne.

Writer-director Seaton, who worked so hard to get *Miracle* made, was rewarded with an Oscar for his work. (The film won three.) Seaton won another seven years later for *The Country Girl*, and went on to write the screenplay for and direct *Airport* in 1970, for which he received another Oscar nomination.

In this chapter, you'll find recipes from six of the film's players, plus one from the studio chief, and delicious toddy with which to wash them all down.

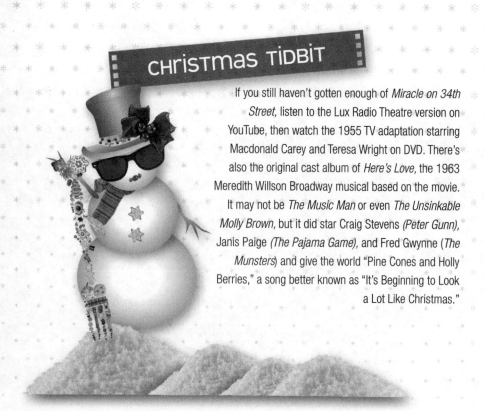

CHRISTMAS TIDBIT

If you still haven't gotten enough of *Miracle on 34th Street,* listen to the Lux Radio Theatre version on YouTube, then watch the 1955 TV adaptation starring Macdonald Carey and Teresa Wright on DVD. There's also the original cast album of *Here's Love,* the 1963 Meredith Willson Broadway musical based on the movie. It may not be *The Music Man* or even *The Unsinkable Molly Brown,* but it did star Craig Stevens *(Peter Gunn),* Janis Paige *(The Pajama Game),* and Fred Gwynne (*The Munsters*) and give the world "Pine Cones and Holly Berries," a song better known as "It's Beginning to Look a Lot Like Christmas."

THeLMa RiTTer, 1902–1969

ONE OF THE WISECRACKING-EST CHARACTER ACTRESSES Hollywood has ever produced, Thelma Ritter made her movie debut in *Miracle on 34th Street* as the world-weary holiday shopper who argues with Santa Claus. "It isn't much of a part," the director told Ritter when he cast her, "but it'll be fun." That it was, and it set Ritter on a path toward six Oscar nominations as Best Supporting Actress.

Audiences didn't have to see, or more importantly, hear the gravel-voiced Ritter twice to remember her. "She had a way with a line that was uproarious," the *New York Times* once said. Ritter sounded like Brooklyn, which was where she grew up. A suburban housewife and sometime radio actress until Hollywood came calling, she went on to do numerous movie roles. Most notably, she played Bette Davis's maid in the 1950 backstage classic *All About Eve*, Richard Widmark's loyal but doomed friend in the 1953 noir *Pickup on South Street*, and Jimmy Stewart's nurse in Alfred Hitchcock's 1954 masterpiece *Rear Window*.

Ritter twice teamed with Doris Day, first playing her housekeeper in the 1959 rom-com *Pillow Talk*, and then portraying her mother-in-law in 1963's *Move Over, Darling*. She also ran the boardinghouse at which Marilyn Monroe liked to stay in 1961's *The Misfits*, and the dedicated mother who lobbied for clemency for her son the inmate (Burt Lancaster) in *Birdman of Alcatraz* in 1962.

Although Ritter never won an Oscar, she holds the record for the most Academy Award nominations in the same category. She did get to cohost the awards with Bob Hope in 1955. And she did receive a Tony Award for the musical *New Girl in Town* in 1958.

Ritter did TV work, too, memorably starring in the 1956 *Alfred Hitchcock Presents* episode "The Babysitter." (It's a really good one!) She was nominated for an Emmy for her work in Paddy Chayefsky's *The Catered Affair,* a 1955 drama broadcast as part of *The Philco-Goodyear Television Playhouse.* Chayefsky maintained that Ritter "was never properly publicly recognized as an actress."

A critic once wrote that Ritter had a face "like a used newspaper." But her everywoman quality is what endeared her to millions. And it all began with *Miracle on 34th Street.* As the story goes, the film's producer Darryl F. Zanuck saw the rushes and was dazzled by her brief moment on screen. As Ritter's *New York Times* obituary said, "She was a hit. After that, it was clear sailing to fame."

Her Seafood Dip will make you a hit at your next holiday party.

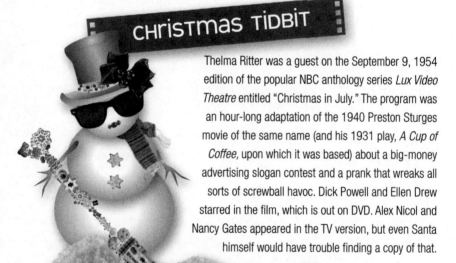

CHRISTMAS TIDBIT

Thelma Ritter was a guest on the September 9, 1954 edition of the popular NBC anthology series *Lux Video Theatre* entitled "Christmas in July." The program was an hour-long adaptation of the 1940 Preston Sturges movie of the same name (and his 1931 play, *A Cup of Coffee,* upon which it was based) about a big-money advertising slogan contest and a prank that wreaks all sorts of screwball havoc. Dick Powell and Ellen Drew starred in the film, which is out on DVD. Alex Nicol and Nancy Gates appeared in the TV version, but even Santa himself would have trouble finding a copy of that.

THeLma RiTTer's seaFOOD DiP

Mix the first five ingredients until well combined. Season, to taste, with soy sauce. Serve with potato chips.

1 (8 ounce) package cream cheese, softened

2 cups sour cream

1 cup mayonnaise or Miracle Whip

½ pound crab meat

1 teaspoon grated onion

Soy sauce, to taste

Jack Albertson, 1907–1981

EFORE HE WAS THE LATTER HALF of *Chico and the Man*, Shelley Winters's (spoiler alert!) widower in *The Poseidon Adventure*, or Charlie's Grandpa Joe in *Willy Wonka & The Chocolate Factory*, Jack Albertson had a tiny uncredited part as a mail sorter in *Miracle on 34th Street*. It was a role—his third picture with no credit actually—that led to a bravura career filled with honors. The man who became *"the Man"* earned a Tony, an Oscar, and three Emmys.

Albertson began his show business career in vaudeville—first as a dancer, then as a straight man to such comics as Phil Silvers, with whom he'd go on to appear in *Top Banana* on Broadway and in the 1954 film version. He made a dozen major movies through the years including 1957's *Man of a Thousand Faces*, the 1961 romantic comedy *Lover Come Back*, and 1962's *Days of Wine and Roses*. His stage work included a legendary West Coast production of *Waiting for Godot* and Neil Simon's hilarious ode to show biz *The Sunshine Boys* on Broadway.

Although Albertson did a tremendous amount of TV acting—appearing on shows from *The Jack Benny Program* to *America 2-Night*—his best-known work was *Chico*, opposite a young comic named Freddie Prinze. Albertson won two Emmys for playing the cantankerous garage owner Ed Brown. He won a third for guest-starring on the *Cher* show. Didn't see that award coming, did you?

Albertson's greatest triumph, though, was playing the father in *The Subject Was Roses*, first on Broadway in 1964 and then on the big screen four years later. He is one of the very few actors to win a Tony and an Oscar for the same role. Martin Sheen, who played the son in the original, took on Albertson's part in a 2010 Los Angeles production. He knew he had big shoes to fill, telling the *New York Times,* "Jack Albertson had this tremendous acting talent. I remember just watching his body shake with emotion during certain lines."

You'll tremble with delight when you taste Albertson's crown roast.

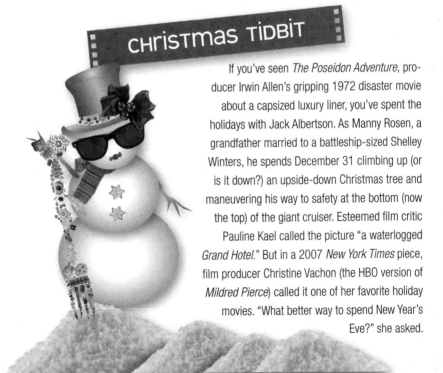

CHRISTMAS TIDBIT

If you've seen *The Poseidon Adventure,* producer Irwin Allen's gripping 1972 disaster movie about a capsized luxury liner, you've spent the holidays with Jack Albertson. As Manny Rosen, a grandfather married to a battleship-sized Shelley Winters, he spends December 31 climbing up (or is it down?) an upside-down Christmas tree and maneuvering his way to safety at the bottom (now the top) of the giant cruiser. Esteemed film critic Pauline Kael called the picture "a waterlogged *Grand Hotel.*" But in a 2007 *New York Times* piece, film producer Christine Vachon (the HBO version of *Mildred Pierce*) called it one of her favorite holiday movies. "What better way to spend New Year's Eve?" she asked.

Jack Albertson's Stuffed Crown Roast of Pork

Serves 8-10

Have your butcher prepare the crown roast of pork. Rinse and dry the roast and cover the ends of the bones with foil. Preheat the oven to 350 degrees. Bake the unstuffed roast for two hours. Meanwhile, marinate the raisins and currants in enough warm Grand Marnier to cover.

In a sauté pan, while roast is cooking, heat oil and slightly brown onion. Add the carrot and celery and cook for a minute or two. Mix these vegetables with the remaining dressing ingredients, including the drained raisins and currants.

Remove the roast from the oven after two hours. Fill the center with the dressing, return it to the oven, and cook the stuffed roast one hour more or until a meat thermometer reaches 175 degrees. Remove roast from oven and let rest for 15 minutes, tented with foil.

Make the sauce by dissolving jelly in a pan over low heat. Add mustard to taste and stir to combine. To serve, remove foil and trim stuffed roast with paper frills. Show it to your guests at the table before removing the stuffing and cutting the meat into chops. Serve the sauce on the side.

1 (8–10 pound) crown roast of pork

Dressing

1 cup raisins

1 cup currants

1 cup (or more) Grand Marnier liqueur

3 tablespoons vegetable oil

¼ cup finely chopped onion

⅓ cup chopped carrots

1 cup chopped celery

2 tablespoons chopped parsley

1 cup (or more) cooked rice

2 teaspoons salt

1 teaspoon pepper

1 teaspoon paprika

¼ teaspoon ground cloves

1 cup crushed pineapple, drained

1 cup shelled pistachios

2 cups dry bread crumbs

Sauce

2 (8–12 ounce) jars red currant jelly

Prepared mustard, to taste

NaTaLie WOOD, 1938–1981 • • • • • ▶

ER FIRST CREDITED ROLE WAS PLAYING Orson Welles's adopted daughter in the 1946 film-noir *Tomorrow Is Forever*. Only a year later, she achieved pop culture immortality as Susan Walker, the precocious eight-year-old who's not quite sure that Santa Claus is real, in *Miracle on 34th Street*. From then on, Natalie Wood enjoyed a meteoric rise in Hollywood.

A brunette beauty of Russian lineage, Wood was cast in *Rebel Without a Cause* at sixteen, played the female lead in the film versions of the two greatest American musicals ever—*West Side Story* and *Gypsy*—by the time she was twenty-four, and was thrice nominated for the Oscar by twenty-five. For someone whose life sadly was cut short (and whose drowning death is still shrouded in mystery), she accomplished an enormous amount. She was even in the 1956 John Ford classic *The Searchers*, considered by many to be the best American Western ever made.

Wood spent the 1960s starring alongside some of Hollywood's handsomest men in such films as *Splendor in the Grass* (opposite Warren Beatty), *Love with the Proper Stranger* (with Steve McQueen), *Sex and the Single Girl* (Tony Curtis), and *Inside Daisy Clover* (Christopher Plummer). She capped off the decade with *Bob & Carol & Ted & Alice,* Paul Mazursky's 1969 comedy-drama about relationships amid the so-called sexual revolution costarring Robert Culp, Elliott Gould, and Dyan Cannon. (I was six when it came out and I still don't get it.)

Wood's greatest pairing—off screen—was with Robert Wagner. She married him twice, once in 1957 and again in 1972. They acted together on occasion, most notably in a TV version of *Cat on a Hot Tin Roof* in 1976. He was Brick, she was Maggie. She also starred in a TV remake of *From Here to Eternity* in 1979 for which she won a Golden Globe. Wood died while her last film, *Brainstorm,* was in production. It was released posthumously in 1983, and while hardly a classic, it gave her fans one last chance to savor her beauty. You'll savor her stroganoff.

cHrisTMas TiDBiT

Natalie Wood and husband Robert Wagner reportedly turned down the chance to remake *Miracle on 34th Street* in the 1970s with Wood's daughter Natasha Gregson Wagner in the role that made her mother famous. Wood said she was too young to be an actress. Almost three decades later, though, Natasha did throw her cap into the Christmas ring as one of the stars of the 2004 TV movie *Angel in the Family.* Directed by actor Georg Stanford Brown and out on DVD, the film tells the story of an ailing widower (Ronny Cox) who can't accept his wife's death. When one of his estranged daughters (not Natasha, the other one) asks for a Christmas miracle, she gets it, and their mother (Meredith Baxter) comes back to life for one more holiday with the gang. Talk about your family ties!

NaTaLie WOOD'S BeeF STroGanoFF

Cut the beef into thin strips and dredge them with flour. In a skillet over medium heat, brown the meat quickly in half the butter. Remove the meat and set it aside. Add the remaining butter to the skillet and sauté the onions and mushrooms for 3 minutes.

Return the meat to the pan. Sprinkle it with salt and pepper. Add the tomato juice, water, and sherry and slowly bring it to a boil. Cover and simmer over low heat, stirring occasionally, until the meat is tender, about 1½ hours. Just before serving, stir in the sour cream and heat through. Serve the stroganoff over rice or egg noodles.

2 pounds sirloin

½ cup flour

¾ cup butter

3 medium onions, chopped

½ pound button mushrooms

Salt and pepper, to taste

1 cup tomato juice

½ cup water

¾ cup sherry

1 cup sour cream

H E WAS FRED MERTZ, the crotchety-but-lovable old goat who was landlord and best friend to Lucy and Ricky Ricardo on *I Love Lucy*, but the crotchety-but-lovable William Frawley also played political adviser Charlie Halloran in *Miracle on 34th Street*. (He advises the judge of the fallout to come if he rules against Santa.)

The classic picture was one of more than a hundred films that Frawley made beginning in—get this!—1916. A vaudevillian who had introduced audiences to the song "My Melancholy Baby," Frawley appeared in both the 1934 and the 1951 versions of *The Lemon Drop Kid*, the latter with Bob Hope; the 1937 Jimmy Cagney starrer *Something to Sing About*; 1939's *The Adventures of Huckleberry Finn* with Mickey Rooney; the 1942 Ginger Rogers picture *Roxie Hart* (which helped inspire the musical *Chicago*); and the well-regarded 1947 comedy *Monsieur Verdoux*, directed and co-written by and starring Charlie Chaplin.

But despite such an amazing film resume, Frawley is best known for the TV work he did as a senior citizen. In his sixties and seventies, he created not only Fred Mertz on *I Love Lucy*, but he was also the housekeeping grandpa Michael Francis "Bub" O'Casey on *My Three Sons*.

During his 1960–65 tenure on the latter program, Frawley was besieged with recipe requests for the Mulligan Stew that Bub was so fond of making. "Of the 34 million people watching *My Three Sons*, 33 million want our recipe," he told *TV Guide* in 1962. He developed one with the help of a newspaperman who loved to cook. "It has everything in it but a leprechaun," Frawley harrumphed in the cantankerous manner for which he will forever be known.

WILLIAM FRAWLEY'S MULLIGAN STEW

Serves 8

Mix the flour with the salt and pepper. Dredge the meat in the seasoned flour. Heat the oil in a Dutch oven and brown the meat in batches. Pour off any excess oil. Return the browned meat to the pan and cover with beef broth. Add the bay leaves, onion, thyme, garlic, allspice, parsley, and salt and pepper. Simmer for two hours. Add your choice of vegetables, preferably a mixture of sliced carrots, diced potatoes, pearl onions, peas, diced tomatoes, and presoaked lentils. Avoid using turnips. Continue to simmer until the meat is tender and the vegetables are cooked. Add the hominy or cooked rice, if desired, and heat through.

3 pounds beef cubes

1 cup flour

1 teaspoon salt

1 cup peanut oil

3 cups beef broth

2 bay leaves

1 medium onion, chopped

1 pinch thyme

2 cloves garlic

6 whole allspice

1 tablespoon parsley

Additional salt and pepper, to taste

2-3 cups vegetables

1 cup canned hominy or cooked rice (optional)

CHRISTMAS TIDBIT

In the 1956 *I Love Lucy* episode known simply as "The Christmas Show," tightwad Fred Mertz (William Frawley) is tickled when he gets a last-minute Christmas tree at half price. But the real thrill comes when he, Ethel, Lucy, and Ricky all dress up as Santa Claus. But who's the guy in the fifth red suit who disappears in a holiday flash? Well, it sure isn't Mrs. Trumbull.

LTHOUGH BEST KNOWN FOR THE ROLE of Santa's attorney Fred Gailey in *Miracle on 34th Street*, John Payne began his career as a radio singer before becoming a movie star in such Fox musicals as 1940's *Tin Pan Alley*, 1941's *Sun Valley Serenade*, and 1943's *Hello, Frisco, Hello*—opposite such legendary leading ladies as Betty Grable, Sonja Henie, and Alice Faye. The famous image of Payne sitting shirtless and legs apart in the corner of a boxing ring in the 1939 comedy-with-music *Kid Nightingale* is one of the sexiest photographs ever taken of a man, period. Google the picture of the half-naked singing boxer. You'll faint.

In 1946, Payne starred with Gene Tierney, Tyrone Power, and Anne Baxter in the drama *The Razor's Edge*, which many feel is among his best work. He didn't sing in that one. Perhaps the baritone got the hint. In the 1950s, Payne let his chest hair grow back in and specialized in playing tough guys in such noirs as *Kansas City Confidential, 99 River Street,* and *Hell's Island*. So much for his Juilliard-trained voice! He turned to television in 1957, playing gun-slinger Vint Bonner in the Western series *The Restless Gun*, which ran for two seasons. Dan Blocker, who became Hoss Cartwright on *Bonanza*, costarred.

In real life, the athletically handsome Payne was married for a time to Anne Shirley, who played Barbara Stanwyck's daughter in *Stella Dallas*, and then to Gloria DeHaven, whose long acting career ran the gamut from *The Thin Man Goes Home* to *B.J. and the Bear*. His third wife was not an actress. Interestingly, Payne grew up in an antebellum mansion and, while wrestling profes-sionally to earn money, studied drama at Columbia University. And, he made a fortune in real estate when acting roles began to wane. Yes, that down-to-earth lawyer from *Miracle on 34th Street* was upper-crusty! Well, smell him!

Better yet, smell his Lamb Casserole with Port Wine. Yum!

JOHN PAYNE'S LAMB CASSEROLE WITH PORT WINE

Preheat oven to 350 degrees. Dip the diced lamb in the port wine. Combine the diced vegetables. In a greased two-quart casserole, arrange the diced lamb in alternating layers with the mixed vegetables and the sliced onions. Season with salt and pepper, to taste. Dip the slices of French bread into the port wine and place atop the casserole. Bake for 1 hour and serve hot.

Serves 6

4 cups diced cooked lamb

1½ cups port wine

2 potatoes, diced

3 carrots, diced

3 stalks celery, diced

1 medium onion, sliced thin

Salt and pepper, to taste

1 loaf of French bread

Darryl F. Zanuck, 1902–1979

ARRYL F. ZANUCK, THE 20TH CENTURY FOX studio chief who gave *Miracle on 34th Street* the green light, knew what he wanted, and what he wanted was to release the picture in May. So what if it was a Christmas movie! The way Zanuck looked at it, more people went to the movies in the summer and that's when box office receipts would be greatest. He left it to the publicity department to downplay the fact that it was holiday fare.

Who could argue with him? The man was larger than life, known for his large cigars and his equally outsized sex drive, and he was one of the first producers to achieve true celebrity status. By 1947, after enjoying a swell run at Warner Brothers, he founded 20th Century Pictures, merged it with Fox, and became one of the most powerful figures in Hollywood. That was an impressive climb for a guy who'd cut his teeth on *Rin Tin Tin*, wouldn't you say?

Before *Miracle on 34th Street*, Zanuck had produced such classics as *Young Mr. Lincoln* and *The Grapes of Wrath* (both starring Henry Fonda), and *How Green Was My Valley* and *The Razor's Edge* with his future *Miracle* stars Maureen O'Hara and John Payne, respectively. He insisted on casting O'Hara in *Miracle* and didn't think the movie could succeed without her. The script, he said, was "excellent, fresh, exciting and delightful," but it needed stars.

A true mogul, Zanuck would go on to produce such stellar hits as *All About Eve* in 1950 and *The Longest Day* in 1962. Over a long career, he won three Irving Thalberg Awards, and his pictures earned numerous Oscars.

His son, Richard D. Zanuck, followed in his footsteps, producing such modern favorites as *Jaws, The Verdict, Cocoon,* and various high-grossing Tim Burton movies. He died in July 2012.

The senior Zanuck offered up his recipe for his favorite chicken dish in 1952. Once you've savored it, feel free to ask your guests, "How great was my curry?"

CHRISTMAS TIDBIT

An extended trailer, available on YouTube, pokes fun at studio chief Darryl F. Zanuck's reluctance to make *Miracle on 34th Street.* In it, actor Chris Tannen plays a thinly veiled version of the executive producer who wonders how any film could be "Hilarious! Romantic! Delightful! Charming! Tender!" and "Exciting!" at the same time. But, of course, *Miracle* is all that and more. Various Fox contract players make cameos. Rex Harrison says *Miracle on 34th Street* is strictly a man's picture. Anne Baxter says she's not sure about that, but she's convinced that women will eat it up. Peggy Anne Garner calls it "groovy" and Dick Haymes says, "This thing is really it." Who can argue with that, Dick?

Darryl F. Zanuck's chicken curry

Sauté the chicken pieces in the butter over medium heat for 20 minutes. Remove the chicken to a plate and add the chopped onions to the pan. Cook until they begin to brown, then add the curry powder and cook for a minute or two. Add the chicken broth and the coconut (or whole) milk and stir to combine. Add the tomatoes and the coconut. Cook for 5 minutes. Return the chicken to the pan and simmer over low heat for 15 minutes or until the chicken is cooked through. Serve the chicken curry over steamed rice with chutney on the side.

Serves 4

2½ pounds chicken, cut into serving pieces

4 tablespoons butter

2 onions, chopped

3 tablespoons curry powder

2 tomatoes, diced

2 tablespoons shredded coconut

1 cup chicken broth

1 cup unsweetened coconut milk (or whole milk)

Steamed rice

Store-bought chutney for serving

BRITISH-BORN EDMUND GWENN is not only the most recognized Santa Claus in all of movie-dom, but he also won an Oscar and a Golden Globe in 1948 for playing the right jolly old elf in *Miracle on 34th Street*. The awards capped an illustrious career as a character actor with such films to his credit as 1935's *Sylvia Scarlett* (as Katharine Hepburn's father), 1940's *Pride and Prejudice* (with Laurence Olivier as Mr. Darcy), 1941's *Charley's Aunt* (in which he woos a cross-dressing Jack Benny), 1943's *Lassie Come Home* (with Elizabeth Taylor), and 1946's *Of Human Bondage*. Amazing for a guy whose father threw him out of the house when he announced that he wanted to be an actor!

In the 1950s, although suffering from arthritis, Gwenn appeared in the classic horror movie *Them!* (featuring James Whitmore and a picnic's worth of giant ants) and the Alfred Hitchcock comedy-thriller *The Trouble with Harry* (starring John Forsythe and Shirley MacLaine). Gwenn had previously worked with Hitch, his fellow Brit, on four films beginning with 1931's *The Skin Game*—reprising the role he'd played in a silent version ten years earlier—and including 1940's *Foreign Correspondent*. He also appeared in an episode of *Alfred Hitchcock Presents* on TV in 1957.

Gwenn did plenty of stage work along the way, too, with roles in everything from Shakespeare to Shaw. Although he could play anything, he almost didn't get to play his most identifiable role. Another actor—Gwenn's cousin, Cecil Kellaway, in fact—had been offered the part of Kris Kringle in *Miracle on 34th Street* first. When he turned it down, Gwenn had Santa in the bag. He gained thirty pounds to play the man in red. It was worth the trouble. When he won his Oscar—the only one ever awarded to an actor playing Father Christmas—Gwenn said, "Now I know there is a Santa Claus." That's sweet, but it still must have sounded like "Up your chimney!" to his fellow nominees that year.

Here's his recipe for holiday cheer. Spike it with a little rum or schnapps and you'll believe in Santa, too.

EDMUND GWENN'S CHRISTMAS CUP

Mix all of the ingredients in a large pot and heat to boiling. Remove from heat and let stand for several hours. Reheat, remove spices, and serve hot.

2 quarts nonalcoholic apple cider

Serves 8-10

¼ cup sugar

8 small pieces of stick cinnamon

12 whole cloves

8 allspice berries

Pinch of salt

3

I'm Dreaming of a White Christmas Cookie

For a movie called *White Christmas*, there's not a lot of snow. Relatively speaking, there's not a lot of Christmas in *White Christmas*, either. What there is, though, is spectacular. The Irving Berlin musical, directed by Michael Curtiz—who'd made, oh, a little picture called *Casablanca*—showcases four amazing performers in peak form: Bing Crosby, Danny Kaye, Rosemary Clooney, and Vera-Ellen. You won't find another quartet more talented or put to better use.

Crosby, of course, was the consummate crooner, "the voice of Christmas," as one of his biographers put it.

Kaye, a former Catskills tummler, was a master of physical comedy who could sing, dance, and act. Clooney couldn't really dance but it didn't matter—she could put a song across better than anyone. Vera-Ellen, no slouch in the looks department, dances like nobody's business. She's been called one of the best dancers ever captured on film. Her voice was dubbed in *White Christmas*, but who's counting? As Clooney said, "If they could have dubbed my dancing, we'd have had a perfect picture."

Filmed in VistaVision—a new high-definition process which helped make *White Christmas* the biggest box office smash of 1954—the movie tells the story of two army buddies (Crosby and Kaye) who, after the war, hit it big as a song-and-dance team. They meet two gorgeous singing sisters (Clooney and Vera-Ellen), and then travel by train from Florida to Vermont to save their favorite general (played by Dean Jagger), who has fallen on hard times. He owns a country inn, with the ever-sassy Mary Wickes at the front desk. But there's no snow, and no snow means no guests. "It used to be a grist mill and a barn," Wickes says. "Now it's a Tyrolean haunted house." The place is ghostly quiet in what should be ski season.

The boys have the answer to his problems, though. They decide to put on a big, splashy show featuring the girls and a giant cast, and invite all their army

Crosby and Vera-Ellen in red for *White Christmas*.

buddies up on Christmas Eve to see it. Everybody drops what they're doing and heads to Vermont, George Chakiris (a future Oscar winner for *West Side Story*) dances up a storm, Crosby and Clooney fall for each other, Kaye and Vera-Ellen make nice, too, and—no surprise!—it finally snows. But wait, there's more.

White Christmas also features the classic quasi-drag number "Sisters," in which Crosby and Kaye roll up their pant legs, toss on a few sparkles, and lip-sync to Clooney and Vera-Ellen's ode to filial unity. Crosby wasn't exactly a cross-dressing kind of guy. But Kaye jumps right in and, sensing that his costar feels weird all dolled up, keeps dinging Bing with a large feather fan until he finally breaks up. It's an honest moment, and it warms up the distant Crosby considerably. It's great to see someone who's always so cool and col-lected actually bust a gut.

There are plenty of other wonderful numbers. Kaye and Vera-Ellen cut loose beside the sea while singing "The Best Things Happen While You're Dancing." Clooney sizzles in a black gown by Edith Head singing "Love You Didn't Do Right by Me" at a New York boite called the Carousel Club, its pink walls evoking the real-life Persian Room. And Clooney and Crosby—who sang in the same key, by the way—perform a gorgeous duet of "Count Your Blessings (Instead of Sheep)." It's just plain lovely to behold them eat-ing sandwiches and drinking buttermilk.

Of course, the title song—sung by Crosby in the beginning and by every-one at the end—seals the deal and makes this beloved film a Christmas clas-sic. "White Christmas," you should know, actually had been introduced in the 1942 Bing Crosby/Fred Astaire musical *Holiday Inn*. It won the Academy Award that year for Best Original Song and proved to be so popular that it got its own movie. We can all be glad it did. When the cast, dressed in red with white fur trim and spangled snowflakes, sings the holiday's best-loved song and those barn doors open to reveal that snow has finally arrived, they know, you know, and I know it's Christmas, and it's as white as any of us could ever hope for.

Here are three of the stars with recipes to delight your holiday guests.

Irving Berlin—a composer whose stature was summed up best by song-writer Jerome Kern's oft-repeated observation, "Irving Berlin has no place in American music. He *is* American music"—began writing what would become "White Christmas" long before the Fred Astaire-Bing Crosby musical *Holiday Inn* endeared it to audiences in 1942.

One story has it that Berlin began writing "White Christmas" on the set of *Top Hat* in 1931. As that version goes, he hummed the tune to Fred Astaire, who liked it, but the film's director Mark Sandrich wasn't blown away. Another story says Berlin wrote the song in 1940 while on holiday in the California desert. That would explain the often-omitted opening bars of the song, which address the singer's longing for a Christmas away from the palm trees of Beverly Hills.

I like the story, whether apocryphal or not, that says Berlin excitedly called his secretary when he came up with "White Christmas" and said, "Grab your pen and take down this song. I just wrote the best song I've ever written! Heck, I just wrote the best song that *anybody's* ever written!" Who's to argue?

When it came time to write the other holiday-themed songs for *Holiday Inn,* which is, in fact, a movie about an inn that opens only on holidays, Berlin borrowed his 1933 composition "Easter Parade." (He also repurposed 1918's "Oh, How I Hate to Get Up in the Morning," but that wasn't holiday-related.)

Berlin easily came up with "Let's Start the New Year Right" and "Let's Say It with Firecrackers," but writing about Christmas, he claimed, was difficult. Whatever it took—and wherever and whenever he did write "White Christmas"—the effort was worth it.

By most accounts, Crosby didn't immediately recognize that the song would become the break-out success of *Holiday Inn,* and he seemed to have no idea that it would go on to be his biggest hit, let alone one of the best-selling records of all time. "I don't think we have any problems with that one, Irving," was about all he said upon first hearing it.

Although "White Christmas" made its official debut in Holiday Inn, Crosby previewed the song on his radio show on Christmas Day 1941. He recorded it the following summer for release on the film's soundtrack. Interestingly, it wasn't the film's first hit song—that honor went to "Be Careful, It's My Heart"—but certainly it is the most enduring. Crosby later decided that he had little to do with the runaway success of "White Christmas." "A jackdaw with a cleft palate could have sung it successfully," he said. But anyone who has heard his recording—and that would be pretty much everyone—knows that humble estimation is for the birds.

ROSEMARY CLOONEY, 1928–2002

LET'S GET THIS OUT OF THE WAY FIRST: Yes, she was the aunt of a certain hunk named George. But the most important thing to know about Rosemary Clooney is not that she had a famous nephew who launched millions of carnal fantasies, but that she had one of the greatest voices of the twentieth century.

Singing professionally since her teens, the Kentucky-born singer-actress found fame in the 1950s via a string of novelty hits including "Come On-a My House" and "Mambo Italiano." Audiences adored these funny little songs, but she wasn't nearly as enamored of them. Clooney wanted to be known as the woman who infused standards like "Hey There" with longing, not the gal who *sang-a* "Botch-a-Me." She wasn't even Italian!

Clooney appeared in *White Christmas,* which would be the pinnacle of her film career, because she knew starring alongside Bing Crosby would lift her stature to new levels. (She's quite clear about that in an interview that accompanies the Blu-ray edition of the film.) Help her career, it did. Not only did Clooney's star turn as girl-singer Betty Haynes in the 1954 film boost her standing in show business, it established her friendship with Crosby. The two later did a concert tour of Ireland together. And Clooney's appearance on a 1978 TV celebration of Crosby's 50th year in show business is considered instrumental in her comeback.

Sadly, Clooney was coming back from a period that hadn't been kind to her. Diagnosed as bipolar, she had a tumultuous relationship with husband José Ferrer—she married, divorced, and remarried him despite his infidelities. He cheated on her on their honeymoon, as the story goes. Their union produced five children, including the talented actor Miguel Ferrer who first made a splash on *Twin Peaks.*

Clooney was appearing on behalf of Robert F. Kennedy when he was assassinated. She had a nervous breakdown shortly thereafter. In the late 1960s, she became addicted to pills. Then in 1976, her sister Betty, with whom she'd performed a sister act early in her career, died suddenly of a brain aneurysm. Worst of all, perhaps, Clooney was becoming known as the jingle-singing spokeswoman for Coronet paper towels rather than as a fabulous jazz performer. She recounts all this in two autobiographies, *This for Remembrance* and *Girl Singer*. Despite all the words, *Publisher's Weekly* said she "remains an enigma."

Clooney died of lung cancer at the too-young age of 74. She'd found love, though, with an old friend later in life and she saw the respect of an audience who appreciates the depth of emotion she brought to songs and who continues to adore (sorry, Rosie, we can't help it) those faux-Italian novelty hits she spiced up so many years ago. Here's a dish from another culture of which Clooney was not a part, Viennese Goulash. You were expecting spaghetti and meatballs? Whatsamattayou?

ROSEMARY CLOONEY'S VIENNESE GOULASH

Serves
6

Using a mortar and pestle, or a small grinder, crush together the marjoram, caraway seeds, lemon rind, and garlic.

In a Dutch oven, melt the butter, add tomato paste and crushed seasoning and stir to combine. Add the sliced onions and, stirring constantly, sauté until golden. Add the paprika and cook for a minute more, stirring constantly. Add the beef, one cup of water, and salt to taste.

Cover and simmer until the beef is tender, about 90 minutes. Add more water during cooking, if needed. Before the goulash is done, add another half cup of water and bring the sauce to a boil. If more sauce is desired, sprinkle the meat with ¼ cup flour and add another cup of water and bring to a boil.

Serve the goulash with egg noodles or boiled potatoes.

- 2 teaspoons marjoram
- 1 teaspoon caraway seeds
- 1 teaspoon finely chopped lemon rind
- 1 clove garlic
- ¾ cup butter
- 1 teaspoon tomato paste
- 2 pounds onions, sliced
- 1 tablespoon sweet Hungarian paprika
- 2 pounds chuck, rump, or round beef, cut into large chunks
- 1½ cups water
- Salt, to taste
- ¼ cup flour, optional

Danny Kaye, 1913–1987

NOBODY COULD DO PATTER ROUTINES like Danny Kaye. Nobody. If there's any question, watch him in the 1956 comedy *The Court Jester* as he tries to remember that "the pellet with the poison's in the flagon with the dragon" and not "the chalice from the palace," because that broke. It's a hilarious bit of business—the go-to clip when anyone wants to discuss Kaye's genius.

The man really could do anything—sing, dance, clown—but he wasn't the first or even the second choice to star opposite Bing Crosby in *White Christmas*. Both Fred Astaire and Donald O'Connor had to turn down the part before it was his. Thank heaven they did! Kaye's number "Choreography" is a scream as it sends up the pretentions of the dance world. And his bayside boogie with Vera-Ellen to "The Best Things Happen While You're Dancing" is a romantic delight.

A Jewish kid from Brooklyn, Kaye got his start in show business working the so-called Borscht Belt. At 20, he joined a vaudeville dance act, touring the United States and then Asia, picking up performance skills on the job. He had a moment in burlesque, made some short films, and then got a break when he appeared in a Broadway show called *Straw Hat Revue* in 1939. Not only was he noticed by the critics, he met his wife, Sylvia, who would go on to write some of his best-loved material, including the patter for which he'd become famous. Kaye's appearance in the 1941 Broadway musical *Lady in the Dark* made him a star.

Three years later, he made his feature film debut in *Up in Arms*. The film was a hit and led to such vehicles as the 1946 boxing comedy *The Kid from Brooklyn*, 1947's *The Secret Life of Walter Mitty* with Boris Karloff (see

Chapter 7), 1949's *The Inspector General,* and the biopics *Hans Christian Andersen* (1952) and *The Five Pennies* (1959) about cornet player "Red" Nichols.

In the 1950s and '60s, Kaye added television to his accomplishments. *The Danny Kaye Show,* which ran from 1963 to 1967, won an Emmy, a Golden Globe, and a Peabody award. The Motion Picture Academy gave Kaye an honorary award in 1955 and the Jean Hersholt Humanitarian Award in 1982, primarily for his decades of work on behalf of UNICEF. Among his TV work, Kaye hosted the Academy Awards in 1952, appeared as himself on *The Lucy Show* in 1964, did a half dozen guest shots on *What's My Line?* in the '60s, and played the Swedish Chef's uncle on a 1978 episode of *The Muppet Show.* Boork, boork, boork, indeed.

Kaye's cooking skills in real life weren't Swedish, but they were impressive. He cooked Chinese food well enough to teach classes in it in his later years. They say he called his kitchen "Ying's Thing." This quick-fix recipe sprang from there. Remember: Don't skimp on the shrimp and clock it when you wok it.

Danny Kaye's Stir-Fried Oysters and Shrimp

Serves 6

1 cup raw oysters

¼ cup flour

Water

½ pound raw shrimp, shelled and deveined

2 tablespoons peanut or vegetable oil

1 two-inch piece of fresh ginger root, peeled and julienned

5 scallions, trimmed and cut into 2-inch pieces

1 teaspoon soy sauce

1 teaspoon sesame oil

Salt, to taste

Freshly ground black pepper, to taste

1½ tablespoons cornstarch

2 tablespoons cold water

Place the oysters in a bowl; add the flour and enough water to cover (this will plunp the oysters). Stir the oysters in the bowl, drain them well, and then rinse them several times with cold water. Drain well.

Bring a pot of water to barely a simmer. Drop oysters into the hot water for 1 minute. Do the same with the shrimp. Do not overcook them.

Heat the oil in a wok over high heat. Add the ginger and scallions and stir-fry for 5 seconds. Add the seafood and stir-fry for 15 seconds. Add soy sauce, sesame oil, salt, and pepper. Blend the cornstarch and the cold water. Pour the cornstarch mixture into the wok and cook it for 10 seconds.

Serve immediately with steamed rice.

BING CROSBY, 1903–1977

HIS NAME WAS HARRY LILLIS CROSBY, but they called him "Bing"—or "Der Bingle" behind German lines. By any name, the man with the bass-baritone and the blue eyes sold hundreds of millions of records, including one of the best-selling singles of all-time, "White Christmas." To say he was popular doesn't begin to tell his story.

Crosby's road pictures with Bob Hope and Dorothy Lamour—*Road to Singapore, Road to Morocco,* and *Road to Bali* among them—were box-office gold between 1940 and 1962. The 1944 musical *Going My Way*, in which Crosby played a young priest, earned him an Oscar. Everyone wanted to see the movie—even Pope Pius XII. The following year, Crosby was nominated again for playing the same character in the sequel, *The Bells of St. Mary's.* That rarely happens. But Crosby was unlike any other.

He got his first taste of show business working as a prop boy at an auditorium in Spokane, WA. As a teenager growing up there, he saw Al Jolson perform and was electrified. Crosby sang in various bands in the 1920s and scored his first big hit with a jazzy rendition of "Ol' Man River." He went solo in the early '30s, quickly garnered a recording contract and a radio show, and was huge in no time. His crooning ushered in a new conversational style that influenced generations of singers.

The song "White Christmas" made Crosby a superstar and forever linked him to the festivities surrounding December 25th. If you grew up in the 1960s and '70s, you saw him on numerous variety shows—he was particularly memorable on *Flip* with Flip Wilson—and on various Christmas specials. On his last telecast, *Bing Crosby's Merrie Olde Christmas*, he sang "The Little Drummer Boy" mashed up with "Peace on Earth" as a duet with David Bowie.

It was a what-are-they-thinking? pairing, even in the strange days of 1970s' variety television. But the 1977 recording became Crosby's last hit. It didn't hurt sales that he died right before the special aired.

Today, that odd medley is a perennial holiday favorite along with Crosby's Christmas songs recorded with the Andrews Sisters—I'm particularly fond of "Mele Kalikimaka"—and of course, "White Christmas."

Crosby's eldest son, Gary, wrote a sort of "Daddy Dearest" tell-all titled *Going My Own Way* after his father's death that accused Bing of emotional abuse—he called him fat—and extreme corporal punishment. His claims didn't really stick, though. Audiences needed to believe—and still do—that the real Bing Crosby was as easygoing as the man up there on the screen. We may never know the whole story, but his cookies are sure to please.

CHRISTMAS TIDBIT

When David Bowie was signed to do Bing Crosby's English-themed 1977 Christmas special, he was supposed to sing "The Little Drummer Boy." But when the Thin White Duke got to the Old White Crooner's set, he announced that he wanted to sing something else. Instead, producers Gary Smith and Dwight Hemion—the guys behind *The Star Wars Holiday Special* (see Chapter 9)—drafted staff composers Ian Fraser and Larry Grossman and writer Buzz Kohan to come up with something to make both *der Bingle* and *der Bowie* happy. In little more than an hour, they wrote "Peace on Earth" and wove it between the pah-rumpa-pum-pums. Some say Crosby didn't know who Bowie was. But as Fraser told the *Washington Post* in 2006, "Bing was no idiot. If he didn't know, his kids sure did."

Bing Crosby's sugar cookies

1¼ cups sugar

2 eggs

⅔ cup vegetable shortening

3 cups flour

2 teaspoons baking powder

1½ teaspoons salt

1 tablespoon orange juice

Grated rind of one orange

Sanding sugar

With an electric mixer, cream together the sugar, eggs, and shortening. Sift the flour, salt, and baking powder together and add to the mixture. Blend on low speed until incorporated. Add the orange juice and grated rind. Beat until smooth and light. Wrap the dough in plastic wrap and chill at least one half hour.

Preheat the oven to 350 degrees. Roll the cookie dough out on a lightly floured board to one-quarter-inch thickness. Cut with cookie cutters, sprinkle with sanding sugar, and bake for 12 to 15 minutes.

56

a Feast of Fabulous Forgotten '40s Features

The 1940s produced more Christmas movies than any other decade. I read that on the Internet. It may or may not be true. Without actually counting them—I was told there would be no math!—I can confidently say that the 1940s produced more *terrific* Christmas movies than any other ten-year span. The '40s gave birth to what may well be the top three Christmas classics of all time: *It's a Wonderful Life* (see Chapter 1), *Miracle on 34th Street* (see Chapter 2), and *Meet Me in St. Louis* (see Chapter 5). That last one is more a Christmas scene, I know, but it's so memorable it counts as a Christmas movie.

Why so many good Christmas movies? Maybe all movies were better back then. Or maybe it had something to do with World War II audiences needing to escape their troubles by watching heartwarming films about the most family-oriented, tradition-bound occasion of the year. Whatever the reason, filmgoing throngs were blessed with sleighfuls of cinematic glitter from Tinseltown.

One of the problems of such a bounty, though, is that a handful of classics (like the three mentioned above) get all the attention, and other films, deserving of just as much adoration, are forgotten by all but the most ardent movie buffs. Everyone has watched a pint-sized Natalie Wood tug on Edmund Gwenn's Santa Claus beard in *Miracle on 34th Street*. But even I've never gotten to see Gene Kelly play a murderer, and Deanna Durbin his knowing lover, in 1944's *Christmas Holiday*, a film noir so dark and sordid that audiences got mad at the stars for appearing in it. (A no-frills DVD is sometimes available for a fortune on the Web.)

The four fabulous forgotten '40s features spotlighted here are easy to find—and you should find them. How many times can you watch *Scrooged*?

First, there's the 1945 comedy *Christmas in Connecticut* starring Barbara Stanwyck. She plays food writer Elizabeth Lane, a writer whose popular

Stanwyck gets a cooking lesson from "Cuddles."

column in *Smart Housekeeping* magazine paints a vivid picture of the Martha Stewart–esque suburban life she leads—only she doesn't. Lane actually lives in a crummy New York City apartment with laundry drying on a line outside on the terrace. (Lose the air-dried blouses and you've got my life, folks.) What's worse, she can't cook. (At least I can do that.)

The charade is nearly blown when sailor Jefferson Jones (Dennis Morgan), whose ship was sunk by the Germans, is rescued. Dehydrated and starving, he wants nothing more than to spend the holidays gorging himself in the bucolic countryside with his favorite food columnist. (How don't-ask-don't-tell is that?) Her publisher (Sydney Greenstreet), eager for the good PR that stunt will bring the magazine, insists the not-so-old salt get his wish. "Where am I going to get a farm?" Lane asks her editor. "I haven't even got a window box!"

Thank heaven for Felix, the restaurateur who, unbeknownst to anyone but Elizabeth and her editor, does all of Lane's cooking. He is played by the zaftig Hungarian actor S. Z. "Cuddles" Sakall. You can't understand a word he says, but he's adorable.

In 1947's *It Happened on Fifth Avenue*, the cops may think the sumptuously appointed mansion belonging to the industrialist and self-made millionaire Michael J. O'Connor (Charles Ruggles) is "as empty as a sewing basket in a nudist camp" every winter, but they'd be wrong. Inside, a good-natured hobo named Aloysius McKeever (Victor Moore) is living the good life, all season long. This year, though, he decides to shelter a group of vets—including Don DeFore and Alan Hale Jr. years before they starred in *Hazel* and *Gilligan's Island*—who are struggling to keep afloat now that they're home from World War II.

Before you know it, O'Connor's beautiful heiress daughter Trudy (Gale Storm) moves in. They think she's just a sheet music salesgirl. Trudy then convinces her father to pose as a park bench–dweller. Aloysius isn't thrilled with the idea—"We can't take in every tramp in New York," he says—but pretty soon homeless Mike (the millionaire) is living there among the poor, too.

Even Mike's ex-wife (Ann Harding) comes back by the end, preparing her former hubby's favorite dish from their lean days. "I must be dreaming. It smells like slumgullion," he says. There are spats aplenty—"You're no Van Johnson yourself," Harding's character tells her ex. "I remember when you had only one chin!"—but love wins out in the end. It has to; it's a Christmas movie.

Harding also starred in another holiday movie that year, *Christmas Eve*, a comedy-drama which brought together three of the decade's hottest leading men: George Raft, George Brent, and Randolph Scott. They play three foster sons—ne're-do-wells all—who must be reunited by December 24 to save eccentric Aunt Matilda (Harding) and her fortune from her nephew's greedy clutches. No one is betting on them, but she's sure her boys will come home. "Christmas Eve," she says. "That's the time when families are together."

Okay, so how eccentric *is* Aunt Matilda? Well, she sets up a toy train on her dining room table to deliver cream to her teatime guests, and she throws birdseed all over her parlor floor, opens the windows, and invites every hungry pigeon in the neighborhood in for lunch. Does the old bat deserve to be locked up and swindled for using a dairy-go-round and serving a birdie buffet? No.

The movie, which was rereleased years later retitled as *Sinner's Holiday*, is no classic, but how many Christmas pictures contain a Nazi interrogation?

Finally, there's my favorite movie of the bunch, *Holiday Affair*, a 1949 romantic comedy starring Robert Mitchum and Janet Leigh. He's a roguish store clerk who really just wants to move to California and build boats; she's the widowed secret shopper who gets him fired from his job. He knows she's a comparison shopper but decides she's too cute to turn in. His floor manager has other ideas and gives him the sack. Wendell Corey is the lawyer who gets the short end of the stick in all matters romantic.

Holiday Affair is sexy. Mitchum plants a wet-and-juicy on Leigh right at the kitchen sink. It's funny. A little kid complains to a toy department Santa, "You didn't bring me the baby brother I asked for last year!" And the movie is just a teensy bit icky, which is refreshing. *Holiday Affair* sparks with Oedipal electricity: Connie Ennis (Leigh) constantly refers to her young son Timmy

(Gordon Gebert) as "Mr. Ennis" and combs his hair to look like her late husband. Yuck.

The little six-year-old isn't up to being the man of the house, but he's very cute, not particularly annoying, and crazy about Steve Mason (Mitchum), so we know he has good taste. Hey, the hunk buys the kid an $80 train set. Who wouldn't love him? Well, Connie at first. But she softens. There's a false arrest, a funny scene with Harry Morgan (Col. Potter from *M*A*S*H!*) as a wisecracking cop, and a satisfying ending for all the characters, even miserable old Wendell.

As the story goes, Howard Hughes, then the head of RKO, persuaded Mitchum to take the role in *Holiday Affair* to soften his bad-boy image and distract audiences from a real-life marijuana bust tarnishing his reputation. Initially, the film wasn't well received, but contemporary audiences have made it a must-watch holiday film whenever it's shown on Turner Classic Movies.

These films have found favor today because they're Christmas movies that aren't solely about Christmas. They're movies populated with funny, good-looking people—emotional films set at a time of year when it's cold out but temperatures are running high, at least in matters of love. This makes them perfect viewing. Make time for them some December—or some July.

BarBara STANWYCK, 1907–1990 ● ● ● ●

cHristmas in connecticut

BARBARA STANWYCK, WHO PLAYED the food columnist in *Christmas in Connecticut*, was as great and beloved an actress as ever there was. If you don't believe me, ask Cecil B. DeMille, Douglas Sirk, Fritz Lang, or Frank Capra. (They're all dead, so you'll have to trust me.)

In such pictures as the heart-wrenching 1937 weepie *Stella Dallas*, the 1939 fight picture *Golden Boy*, and the 1944 noir classic *Double Indemnity*, she demonstrates amazing versatility. I particularly love her in the two pictures she made for Sirk—*All I Desire* in 1953 and *There's Always Tomorrow* in 1956, which reunited her with Fred MacMurray, her *Double Indemnity* costar.

Her filmography includes such terrific pictures as 1941's *Meet John Doe* and *The Lady Eve*; 1946's *The Strange Love of Martha Ivers*; *Sorry, Wrong Number* in 1948; and *Clash by Night* in 1952. Stanwyck was as delicious as her character names when she played Sugarpuss O'Shea in 1941's *Ball of Fire* and Dixie Daisy in 1943's *Lady of Burlesque*, too.

In 1960, her TV anthology series, *The Barbara Stanwyck Show*, earned the actress her first Emmy Award. And then came *The Big Valley*. As frontier matriarch Victoria Barkley—picture Lorne Greene in a prairie dress—Stanwyck became a star for a whole new generation, and picked up her second Emmy.

It was a particularly good acting job considering that Stanwyck (née Ruby Stevens) was a former Ziegfeld dancing girl from Brooklyn, New York. Linda Evans, her *Big Valley* costar, praised her work and her decency. Evans once told me that Stanwyck made it a point to learn the names of everyone on the set—in front of the cameras and behind the scenes—and to show a genuine interest in their lives. It is no wonder that she was adored.

Stanwyck's final TV hurrahs were in the miniseries *The Thorn Birds*, which earned her a third Emmy, and the *Dynasty* spinoff *The Colbys*, which didn't earn her much besides her salary. (It wasn't very good.) But throughout a 60-year career, she remained as fresh as her Christmas Kipfels.

Barbara Stanwyck's Christmas Kipfels

Serves
8

1 cup butter, softened

1 cup cream cheese, softened

1 tablespoon sour cream

1 pinch salt

2 cups flour

1½ cups raspberry or apricot jam

Blend butter, cream cheese, sour cream, and salt until creamy. Sift in flour. Mix and knead until smooth. Gather it up into a ball, wrap in plastic wrap or wax paper, and chill at least three hours.

Preheat oven to 350 degrees. Roll out the dough very thin, and cut it into 3-inch squares. Spread each square with 1 tablespoon jam. Roll squares from corner to corner, and shape into crescents. Bake on a greased cookie sheet for 20 minutes. Carefully transfer to a rack and let cool. Makes 24 cookies.

I FIRST LAID EYES ON CHARLES RUGGLES on a 1965 episode of *The Munsters*. As a nearsighted justice of the peace, he tried to marry Herman and Grandpa when they showed up in his backwater town hall looking for a driver's license. Think of it! They could've made history! Oh well.

Ruggles, of course, had had a long career by then. He made nearly a hundred pictures, including the 1936 screen version of *Anything Goes* starring Ethel Merman and Bing Crosby, Howard Hawks's classic 1938 rom-com *Bringing Up Baby* with Katharine Hepburn and Cary Grant, and the Disney movies *The Parent Trap, Son of Flubber, The Ugly Dachshund,* and *Follow Me, Boys!* in the 1960s.

Although his initial career path was leading him toward a life in medicine, Ruggles made the leap to acting. By the second decade of the 1900s, he was appearing on Broadway. In the 1920s, he divided his time between the stage and silent pictures, and then made the leap to talkies in 1929 when he appeared as a drunken newspaperman in *Gentlemen of the Press*. He was one of the stars of 1935's *Ruggles of Red Gap*, although he played a Floud rather than a Ruggles, opposite his frequent costar Mary Boland. For the record, Ruggles did play a character named Charlie Ruggles in a forgotten 1949 TV series called, yes, *The Ruggles*.

Ruggles—the real one—won a 1959 Tony Award as a featured actor in the Broadway comedy *The Pleasure of His Company*. He played the role in the 1961 movie version starring Fred Astaire, too. In his later years, he appeared on various sitcoms including *Bewitched* (as a warlock beau of Aunt Clara's), *The Beverly Hillbillies* (as father-in-law to banker Millburn Drysdale), and

The Andy Griffith Show, as suitor to a certain plump frump in the 1965 episode "Aunt Bee, The Swinger."

At Christmastime, though, it's best to remember Ruggles in *It Happened on Fifth Avenue* as the rich industrialist who regains his humanity—and his wife's love—by joining the ranks of the poor. How fun to watch a crotchety

Ruggles, Harding, and a pot of slumgullion.

old moneybags forced to live in the servants' quarters of his own home—you have to see the movie to see how he gets there—and share his rickety bed with a dog!

If only such a lesson could be taught to Donald Trump.

Wherever you discover (or discovered) Ruggles's work, it's only here that you'll find his recipe for cauliflower and mushroom casserole.

CHARLES RUGGLES'S CAULIFLOWER AND MUSHROOM CASSEROLE

Steam the cauliflower until crisp-tender. Break it into pieces and place it in a buttered casserole.

Preheat the oven to 350 degrees. In the top of a double boiler, melt the butter. Sauté the mushrooms and onion until soft but not brown. Add the flour, salt, and pepper to the mushrooms and onions; stir and cook for 1 minute. Slowly add the milk and cook until thickened. Pour this over the cauliflower. Bake the casserole for 15 minutes.

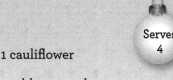

Serves 4

1 cauliflower

2 tablespoons butter, plus more for greasing casserole dish

1 cup sliced mushrooms

1 teaspoon grated onion

2 tablespoons flour

¼ teaspoon salt

⅛ teaspoon pepper

1 cup milk

Dennis Morgan, 1908–1994

HIGH ON THE HOLIDAY HOT-O-METER, Dennis Morgan was one of the top leading men at Warner Brothers in the 1940s. He began his career doing bit parts but broke into the big time with the 1940 Ginger Rogers favorite *Kitty Foyle*. In the years that followed, he appeared in such films as *Captains of the Clouds* with James Cagney, *My Wild Irish Rose* with Arlene Dahl, and *God Is My Co-Pilot* with Raymond Massey.

Hoping to come up with another Hope-and-Crosby duo, the studio cast Morgan in a series of buddy pictures like 1946's *Two Guys from Milwaukee* and 1948's *Two Guys from Texas* with Jack Carson (who was so good at getting on Joan Crawford's nerves in *Mildred Pierce*). But those films didn't stand the test of time the way the holiday favorite *Christmas in Connecticut* has. Morgan makes as winning a food-obsessed seaman as there ever was.

Although he once said, "It's not the easiest thing in the world to be a success in Hollywood and still be the ordinary husband and father," Morgan was married in real life more than sixty years to the same woman. They had three kids.

Although he did television in the 1950s—most notably a 1958 episode of *Alfred Hitchcock Presents*—Morgan pretty much gave up the business after that. He did do a few guest shots here and there, though. His final roles were in the big-screen yearbook of Old Movie Stars called *Won Ton Ton, the Dog Who Saved Hollywood,* and on television in *The Love Boat*.

Considering that many of us first discovered him on the high seas in *Christmas in Connecticut*, it seems like a fitting way for Morgan to have gone out.

His stuffed steak will float your boat.

Dennis Morgan's Stuffed Steak

Preheat the oven to 325 degrees. Mix the bread crumbs with ½ cup of water, and then add salt, pepper, chopped celery, and onion. Spread this crumb mixture on the steak, then roll up. Tie with cooking twine.

Place the turnips and carrots in a roasting pan. Place the meat on top of the vegetables. Pour in 2 cups of water, cover the pan with foil, and bake the steak for 2½ to 3 hours. Let it rest for 10 minutes, remove the twine, and then slice into rounds.

1 (2 pound) round steak, no more than 1 inch thick

1 turnip, diced

1 carrot, diced

1 cup bread crumbs

Water

1 teaspoon salt

¼ teaspoon pepper

¾ cup finely chopped celery

1 tablespoon finely chopped onions

IT Happened on FiFTH avenue

HER STAGE NAME MADE HER SOUND like bad weather. But on television in the 1950s, singer/ actress Gale Storm was all sunshine. From 1952 to 1955, she starred on *My Little Margie*, a summer replacement for *I Love Lucy*, which proved so popular that it continued for three more seasons. Silent-film star Charles Farrell played her dad. *Margie*'s success led in 1956 to The *Gale Storm Show*, which co-starred another pre-talkie talent, ZaSu Pitts, and ran for four seasons.

Storm's other TV work included one-shot appearances on *Burke's Law, The Love Boat,* and *Murder, She Wrote*. Certainly, these were better-quality vehicles than some of the movies in which she appeared in the decade before *My Little Margie* made her a household name. Among Storm's credits are *Freckles Come Home, Sunbonnet Sue, Revenge of the Zombies,* and *Cosmo Jones, Crime Smasher*.

It Happened on Fifth Avenue was one of the few exceptions to the string of dubious film projects with which Storm was saddled. The holiday film, along with *The Dude Goes West* in 1948 and *The Underworld Story* in 1950, was worthy of her talents. Storm was also known as a singer—in fact, she had a million-seller with a cover version of "I Hear You Knockin'." But for whatever reason, she did not do her own singing in *It Happened on Fifth Avenue*. (The voice that comes out of her mouth in the sheet music store actually comes as a bit of a shock.)

In her 1981 autobiography, *I Ain't Down Yet*, Storm recounted how a Texas girl born Josephine Cottle became a TV star named Gale Storm—as a teenager, she won the talent contest *Gateway to Hollywood*, which came with a one-year movie contract and a new name—and how she overcame her struggles with alcoholism. Today, the best of her music is on CD, episodes of *My Little Margie* are on DVD, and every Christmas she gets her man, Don DeFore, in *It Happened on Fifth Avenue*. Storm has subsided, but her star is still shining. Here's her greatest kitchen hit.

Gale Storm's Chicken Cacciatore and Noodles Parmesan

Broil the chicken breasts until done. Cool and debone. Slice the green onions, mushrooms, and black olives and then sauté them in a skillet until soft but not brown. Add the tomatoes and the tomato sauce. Season the mixture with the bay leaf, salt and pepper, oregano, and garlic.

Add the chicken and simmer for 45 minutes.

Cook the egg noodles according to package directions. Mix together the sauce ingredients. Drain the noodles, return them to the pan, and toss with the sauce.

Serve the chicken cacciatore over the noodles.

Serves 4

Chicken

4 chicken breasts

4 green onions

½ pound mushrooms

1 small can black olives

1 can whole spiced tomatoes

1 small can tomato sauce

1 bay leaf

Salt and pepper to taste

1 teaspoon oregano

1 clove garlic

Noodles

2 cups wide egg noodles

½ cup sour cream

¼ teaspoon garlic salt

Salt and pepper, to taste

¼ cup butter, melted

3 tablespoons Parmesan cheese

DON DeFORE, 1913–1993

ON DEFORE IS BEST KNOWN as George "Mr. B" Baxter, the man who employed—and, more importantly, tolerated—the mischievous domestic Hazel Burke, played by Shirley Booth (see Chapter 8), on the popular 1960's sitcom *Hazel*. Before that, he was the Nelsons' neighbor "Thorny" on *The Adventures of Ozzie and Harriet* in the 1950s.

Although thought of as a TV actor, DeFore appeared in numerous films, working for such esteemed directors as Mervyn LeRoy (1944's *Thirty Seconds Over Tokyo*), Michael Curtiz (1948's *Romance on the High Seas*), and Douglas Sirk on at least three movies, including 1957's *Battle Hymn*.

DeFore's other films include 1942's *The Male Animal*, the 1946 John Wayne picture *Without Reservations*, the 1949 Martin-and-Lewis comedy *My Friend Irma*, and the 1950 noir *Dark City* starring Charlton Heston. His role as the down-on-his-luck ex-Army man Jim Bullock who falls for an heiress (Gale Storm) in *It Happened on Fifth Avenue* showed off DeFore's romantic side, and proved that he looked pretty darn good in boxers. He's wearing them when he handcuffs himself to his bed to keep from being evicted. It doesn't work.

In his later years, DeFore did occasional guest roles on such series as *Marcus Welby, M.D.; Fantasy Island; Vega$; Murder, She Wrote;* and *St. Elsewhere*. He was a family man in real life—a father of five who was married to the same woman for more than half a century—and he was most believable cast in such roles. DeFore's recipe for Cheese Fondue Casserole is appropriately homespun, and as Hazel would say, it's a real "doozy" if you like cheese.

DON DeFore's CHEESE FONDUE CASSEROLE

Serves
2

Preheat the oven to 350 degrees. Grease a casserole dish. Mix the milk and cheese in a double boiler over simmering water, stirring frequently, until the cheese is melted. When the milk and cheese are incorporated, remove the mixture from the heat and stir in the beaten eggs. Season it with the salt, mustard, and paprika. Place the bread in the casserole dish and pour the cheese sauce over it. Bake the casserole for 25 minutes or until set.

1 cup milk

1 cup grated cheese

2 eggs, beaten

1 tablespoon butter

½ teaspoon salt

½ teaspoon mustard

Paprika, to taste

1 cup bread, torn into pieces

JOAN BLONDELL, 1906–1979

christmas eve

IF YOU KNOW JOAN BLONDELL simply from *Here Come the Brides*—she played Lottie Hatfield on the lighthearted Western in the late 1960s—or from her appearance in *Grease* in 1978, you don't know the half of it.

Beginning in the 1930s, Blondell specialized in playing the blonde wiseacre, and in pre-Code Hollywood, few were better at it. A beauty queen in the 1920s—she came in fourth in the Miss America pageant—Blondell appeared in such films as the classic 1931 James Cagney crime drama *The Public Enemy* and the Busby Berkeley musical *Gold Diggers of 1933*.

In the years that followed, she stretched her wings in the 1945 Elia Kazan film *A Tree Grows in Brooklyn*, the 1947 Tyrone Power noir *Nightmare Alley*, and the 1951 drama *The Blue Veil*, for which she was Oscar nominated. Not to mention her small-but-memorable role in *Christmas Eve* in which she throws expensive gifts out the window of a hotel and drives away her boyfriend's fiancée.

In the '50s, Blondell alternated between TV appearances and roles in such kitschy film favorites as *The Opposite Sex* (the 1956 musical version of *The Women*) and *Will Success Spoil Rock Hunter?*, the Frank Tashlin comedy starring Jayne Mansfield. Blondell was in the Tracy-Hepburn favorite *Desk Set*, too.

There seemed little question that Blondell would go into show business. She was born into a vaudeville family. (Her father was a Katzenjammer Kid!) But few would have imagined that in her sixties and seventies, she'd be doing some of her best work. Critics raved about her performance in Norman Jewison's 1965 poker picture, *The Cincinnati Kid*, and in John Cassavetes' 1977 show-business drama *Opening Night*. She'd do serious movies like these and then appear on *The Snoop Sisters* and *Starsky and Hutch*. I love that.

With the recipe that follows, you can ham it up, too

JOAN BLONDELL'S BUFFET HAM

Begin the day before you want to serve the ham. Wash the ham, put it in a large stockpot, cover it with boiling water, and simmer it over low heat for 4 hours. Remove the ham from the heat, cover, and let it cool to room temperature in the water. It can stand overnight at room temperature.

The following morning, remove the ham from the water (reserving 3 tablespoons of the water) and remove the fatty rind from the ham. Make slashes across the surface of the ham—cut in two directions to create a traditional diamond pattern—and stick the whole cloves into the ham where the slashes intersect.

Preheat the oven to 400 degrees. Make a paste of the sugar, flour, mustard, syrup, and cooking water. Place the ham in a roasting pan and spread the paste over it. Bake the ham uncovered for 45 minutes. Remove it from the oven, wait 10 minutes, then slice and serve.

Serves 12

1 (10 pound) uncooked ham

1 cup brown sugar, packed

½ cup flour

Whole cloves

1 teaspoon dry mustard

½ cup maple syrup

3 tablespoons water

I FIRST SAW REGINALD DENNEY IN HIS LAST FILM ROLE. He was playing Commodore Schmidlapp in the big-screen spinoff of the TV series *Batman* in 1966. By then, he had been acting for almost 60 years and been an amateur boxing champion and a stunt pilot, too. What can I say except, better to discover him late than never.

Born into a British show business family—his father sang Gilbert and Sullivan with the best of them—Denny began his career while still in his teens. He made the leap from stage to silent films in 1919, and continued to make pictures for the rest of his life. Among his best-known are the 1934 drama *Of Human Bondage*, the 1940 Hitchcock mystery *Rebecca*, the 1948 Cary Grant rom-com *Mr. Blandings Builds His Dream House*, and the 1965 Western comedy *Cat Ballou*.

Denny's other movies include the 1931 film version of Noel Coward's *Private Lives*, the 1935 *Anna Karenina* starring Greta Garbo, 1942's *Captains of the Clouds* starring James Cagney and Dennis Morgan (also featured in this chapter), and the 1947 Bob Hope detective spoof *My Favorite Brunette* with Dorothy Lamour. You can even see Denny in 1953's *Abbott and Costello Meet Dr. Jekyll and Mr. Hyde*—but don't put it on the top of your must-watch list.

In his day, Denny's interest in model airplanes and aeronautics were as well documented by the press as his acting. During World War II, he even had a contract with the U.S. Army. But it's his acting we remember. Few could play the stiff-upper-lipped Brit better than he could. His recipe for broiled lobster tails is appropriately hifalutin.

REGINALD DENNY'S BROILED LOBSTER TAILS

Marinate frozen lobster tails in the lemon juice until they reach room temperature. Drain them and then coat them with melted butter and broil until they're golden.

To make the sauce, melt 3 tablespoons butter in a saucepan over low heat. Stir in the flour and cook for a moment. Add the wine, heavy cream, parsley, minced onion, salt, and pepper. Stir to combine. Blend in the beaten egg yolks and heat through, but take care to remove from the heat before the yolks begin to cook.

Top each lobster tail with the sauce and serve.

Lobster

6 (4 ounce) frozen rock lobster tails

1 cup fresh lemon juice

½ stick melted butter

Sauce

3 tablespoons butter

3 tablespoons flour

½ cup dry white wine

1½ cups heavy cream

1 teaspoon chopped parsley

1 teaspoon dry minced onion

Salt and pepper, to taste

3 egg yolks, lightly beaten

a FEAST OF FABULOUS FORGOTTEN '40s FEATURES

George Brent, 1899–1979

GEORGE BRENT MADE HIS FILM DEBUT in 1930's *Under Suspicion.* The Irish-born actor, who first came to America with a touring production of *Abie's Irish Rose* in the mid-1920s, went on to win the distinction in Hollywood of being Bette Davis's favorite leading man. They made more than a dozen pictures together, including the classics *Jezebel* in 1938 and *Dark Victory* in 1939.

Brent's other leading ladies ran the gamut from Greta Garbo in 1934's *The Painted Veil* to Yvonne De Carlo in 1947's *Slave Girl.* Barbara Stanwyck, Lucille Ball, Claudette Colbert—Brent starred with them all. (They say he was popular with the ladies off screen, too.) His best-loved pictures include the 1933 Busby Berkeley musical *42nd Street* and the 1945 thriller *The Spiral Staircase.*

As the empty-pocketed playboy Michael in *Christmas Eve,* whose girlfriend (Joan Blondell) loves him more than she should, Brent made his contribution to the holiday genre. The movie may not be his finest hour—it's certainly not up there with the best of the Bette Davis pictures—but it'll introduce you to Brent's oeuvre.

Here's his recipe for "Saratoga Potatoes." Today, we call them potato chips.

George Brent's Saratoga Potatoes

Serves 6

3 large white potatoes

Olive oil, for frying

Sea salt

Peel and then carefully slice the potatoes as thin as possible, preferably using a mandolin. Soak the slices in cold water for 20 minutes, then place in fresh ice water.

Pour a half inch of the oil into a sauté pan and heat to 380 degrees.

Drain a few potato slices at a time and pat dry with a paper towel. Lower the potato slices into the hot oil and cook until just beginning to color. Several minutes on each side should do it. Drain them in a single layer on baking sheets lined with paper towels, and keep them warm in a 175-degree oven until all the potatoes are cooked. Before serving, sprinkle them with salt.

HOLIDAY AFFAIR

BY THE TIME SHE WAS HACKED TO BITS in a motel shower by a not-very-hospitable front desk clerk in *Psycho* in 1960—a role that would win her a Golden Globe award and an Oscar nomination for Best Supporting Actress— Janet Leigh had been a Hollywood beauty to be reckoned with for a dozen years.

Discovered in 1945 by actress Norma Shearer and dubbed "Hollywood's No. 1 Glamour Girl" in 1948, Leigh starred in such films as the 1949 version of *Little Women*, the 1955 musical *My Sister Eileen*, and the 1958 Orson Welles thriller *Touch of Evil*, which is the nuts if you like gritty film noir. In *Holiday Affair*, two men fight for her affections. It was no wonder why. Leigh was gorgeous!

Of Danish heritage, she famously married Tony Curtis in 1951. Their union produced not only actress (and yogurt spokesperson) Jamie Lee Curtis, but also five films in which they costarred, including the 1953 biopic *Houdini*. None were the best films of either star's career.

Much later, Leigh costarred with her daughter in the horror films *The Fog* in 1980 and *Halloween H20: Twenty Years Later* in 1998. Among her other notable films are the 1951 baseball comedy *Angels in the Outfield*, the brutal 1953 Western *The Naked Spur*, the classic 1962 political thriller *The Manchurian Candidate*, the 1963 film version of the Broadway musical *Bye Bye Birdie*, and the 1966 Paul Newman mystery *Harper*.

Like so many actors, Leigh segued into television in the late 1960s. From then until her death, she did parts here and there—a *Columbo*, a *Love Boat*, a *Touched by an Angel*. But we remember her best from the films in which she was victimized—*Psycho, Touch of Evil, The Naked Spur*—and once a year, for the kinder, gentler time she had falling for Robert Mitchum. Together, they turned a *Holiday Affair* into what audiences hoped would be a lifetime of happiness.

In real life, Leigh married four times. (Curtis was her second husband.) Although she didn't seem to have a lot of alone time, her recipe is for one.

JANET LEIGH'S INDIVIDUAL CHEESE SOUFFLé

Melt the butter in a sauce pan. Stir in the flour, salt, and cayenne pepper. Pour in the milk and stir over low heat until the mixture thickens. Do not let it boil. Remove the pan from the heat and stir in the Parmesan cheese. Add the mustard and the beaten egg yolk and stir. Fold in the beaten egg white.

Preheat the oven to 375 degrees. Spread the Liederkranz or Limburger cheese on the piece of toasted whole wheat bread, and place it in the bottom of a greased single-serving casserole dish. Pour the egg mixture over the toast.

Bake for 20 minutes without opening the oven door. Serve immediately.

Serves 1

1 tablespoon butter

1 tablespoon flour

Pinch of salt

Pinch of cayenne pepper

½ cup whole milk

1 tablespoon grated Parmesan cheese

½ teaspoon mustard

1 egg yolk, beaten

1 egg white, stiffly beaten

2 tablespoons Liederkranz or Limburger cheese

1 slice of whole wheat bread, toasted

ROBERT MITCHUM WAS A COOL CAT and a real Hollywood he-man who became an actor only as a last recourse. He spent much of his early life being what used to be called a "delinquent." His bad-boy reputation was hard-won. He was expelled from schools, he did time on a chain gang, he had a nervous breakdown—the man did it all and survived! He took his tough-as-nails street cred and parlayed it into a fantastic career playing prototypical antiheroes in the movies.

He started as a villain in *Hopalong Cassidy* movies in the early 1940s, then segued into war pictures, including 1944's *Thirty Seconds Over Tokyo*. Noir films came next, like Jacques Tourneur's 1947 classic *Out of the Past* and Don Siegel's 1949 *The Big Steal*. *Holiday Affair* was a bit of a switch for Mitchum.

In the 1950s, Otto Preminger cast him as an ambulance driver in 1952's *Angel Face*; actor-turned-director Charles Laughton gave him the chilling role of a religious fanatic in the 1955 cult favorite *Night of the Hunter*, and John Huston shipwrecked him with a nun (Deborah Kerr) in 1957's *Heaven Knows, Mr. Allison*.

Mitchum worked steadily in films throughout the 1960s and '70s. Among his best-known works are the thriller *Cape Fear* in 1962 and David Lean's 1970 epic *Ryan's Daughter*. He played Philip Marlowe in 1975's *Farewell, My Lovely* and 1978's *The Big Sleep*, too. Focusing on television in the '80s, Mitchum made appearances in two miniseries, *North and South* and *War and Remembrance*. He also played the role of a police lieutenant in the 1991 remake of *Cape Fear*. How cool is that?

When asked for a holiday recipe back in 1970, Mitchum offered up his eggnog for a crowd. "I make no apology for the excessive quantity," Mitchum told the food writer who'd requested the recipe. "Only a dope would go to the trouble for less." It'll be perfect for any holiday affair you might throw.

ROBEᴙT MITCHUM'S EGGNOG

Beat egg yolks and confectioners' sugar together in a large bowl. Beat in the rum, brandy, or whiskey. Add cream and milk. In a separate bowl, beat egg whites with salt until stiff but not dry. Fold this mixture into the liquid. Chill.

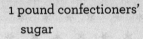

Serves 20

12 egg yolks

1 pound confectioners' sugar

1 quart rum, brandy, or whiskey

2 quarts cream

1 quart milk

12 egg whites

½ teaspoon salt

wenDell corey, 1914–1968

H E PLAYED A DISTRICT ATTORNEY in love with jewel thief Barbara Stanwyck in 1950's *The File on Thelma Jordan,* a detective in Alfred Hitchcock's classic 1954 thriller *Rear Window,* and a blackmailing studio executive in the corrosive 1955 Hollywood exposé *The Big Knife.* But whenever I think of Wendell Corey, it's as the boring-but-loyal guy who *doesn't* get

Mitchum, Leigh, and Corey sup with the cast of *Holiday Affair.*

the girl in *Holiday Affair*, and the doormat of a husband who lets his house-proud beyotch-of-a-wife Joan Crawford walk all over him in *Harriet Craig*, one of the best movies that's not yet on DVD.

If you ask me, Corey was sharpest at playing dull.

The son of a New England clergyman, Corey began his acting career in summer stock in the 1930s, but graduated to Broadway roles by the early '40s. He was noticed as a cynical newsman in the 1945 comedy *Dream Girl*, and soon found himself under contract at Paramount. He played a gangster in his first film, 1947's *Desert Fury* starring Burt Lancaster. They appeared together again in the taut 1948 thriller *Sorry, Wrong Number* starring Stanwyck.

Corey continued to find a lot of work in Hollywood, easing his way from film to television as that new medium took hold. He starred in a number of TV series in the 1950s and early '60s—*Harbor Command, Peck's Bad Girl, Westinghouse Playhouse,* and *The Eleventh Hour*—but none lasted more than a season. Sadly, Corey died young, his career—and life—curtailed by alcoholism. His last film, released only months before his death, was an exploitation flick called *The Astro-Zombies*. If his liver hadn't given out, he might have died of embarrassment.

wenDeLL corey's New engLanD BoiLeD Dinner

Bring the water to a boil in a large stockpot. Cut the salt pork into small slices. Add the rump roast and salt pork to the water. Lower the heat to simmer. Cook the meat for 2 hours, skimming occasionally. Then add one of the onions, whole, studded with the three cloves. Chop the leeks, parsley, and celery, and add them to the pot, too. Cook for another 2 hours.

While this is cooking, core and quarter the cabbage. Peel the potatoes. Cut the carrots, turnip, potatoes, and remaining onions into medium-sized pieces. After the meat has been cooking for a total of four hours, add the vegetables to the pot. Cook everything for an additional 25 minutes or until the potatoes are done.

Serve the meat on a large platter surrounded by the vegetables. Serve the horseradish as an accompaniment.

8 quarts water

1 (6 pound) rump roast

1 pound salt pork

4 onions

3 cloves

2 leeks

½ bunch parsley

1 bunch celery

1 head of cabbage

1 pound carrots

1 turnip

3 medium potatoes

Horseradish

5

eat meat in ST. LOUIS

I t is one of the greatest movie musicals of all time, the first to seamlessly incorporate songs into the action, making it as revolutionary for the big screen as *Oklahoma* was for the stage. But if you ask me, the Smiths—the turn-of-the-last-century family at the center of Vincente Minnelli's 1944 classic *Meet Me in St. Louis*—are just plain weird.

What a fuss they make over a World's Fair coming to Missouri, and that isn't the half of it! For these kooks, a long-distance phone call during a corned-beef-and-cabbage dinner is a thrill of a lifetime. The answer to a fat lip is to send Judy Garland next door to bite her neighbor in retaliation. A trolley ride isn't just a mode of transportation; it's a hormone-fueled frenzy that gets hotter with each clang-clang-clang. Thank God the subway isn't like this!

When it comes to the holidays, the Smiths get even stranger.

On Halloween, the family's morbid little six-year-old girl Tootie (Margaret O'Brien)—a Wednesday Addams–esque tomboy who buries her dolls in the yard—builds a fire in a street, and then pranks some fat bastard down the block by ringing his doorbell, screaming "I hate you!" when he answers, and throwing a handful of flour in his face. And the kid got an Oscar for this!

Christmas is just as bizarre at their house. Esther Smith (Garland) considers her life almost ruined when her boyfriend's tuxedo is locked inside a closed tailor shop and she has to go to the big holiday dance with her grandfather instead. Patriarch Alonzo, a banker played by Leon Ames, is told he's being transferred to New York City and, instead of being elated, the entire clan becomes shrouded in melancholy by the thought of leaving St. Louis. (Honestly? They didn't even have an arch then!)

By the time Judy finishes singing "Have Yourself a Merry Little Christmas" to her little sister, even Santa is ready to slash his wrists. What does Tootie do that night? She goes outside and decapitates all the snowmen the

O'Brien and Garland in *St. Louis*.

family has built. I don't care if that is how they celebrated Christmas in 1904. These people are nuts.

That said, Liza Minnelli—daughter of Judy Garland and the film's director—calls *Meet Me in St. Louis,* in the introduction to the 2011 Blu-ray release, her "favorite holiday movie" and perhaps her favorite of all her mother's movies. And while considerably different from the film, a stage version of the musical ran on Broadway in 1989–90 and has become a perennial favorite in theatres around the country at Christmastime. So it's clear that people do relate to this story.

It's interesting to note, though, that in real life, the family *did* move to New York and never went back to St. Louis to see the fair. The stories by Sally Benson upon which the film was based appeared in the *New Yorker* rather than the *St. Louis Post-Dispatch.* Maybe the real Smiths weren't so weird. Hollywood was.

S HE WAS BORN FRANCES GUMM into a family of vaudevillians. But to generations of film and concert audiences, she was (and is) the often imitated (but ultimately inimitable) Judy Garland, one of the greatest and most heartbreaking stars that Hollywood ever produced.

The actress who would become Dorothy Gale, the young Kansas girl who traveled via tornado to the magical Land of Oz in the timeless 1939 fantasy *The Wizard of Oz*, was discovered by studio mogul Louis B. Mayer in 1935. She got her start in *Pigskin Parade*, a 1936 musical featuring her future *Oz* costar Jack Haley, and by the time she was 17, she was a megastar—and the biggest gay icon ever. All it took was one listen to "Over the Rainbow" and audiences were hooked.

Longing to do work with more substance than the *Andy Hardy* movies in which she'd been appearing, a quickly maturing Garland appeared in such popular films as *For Me and My Gal* in 1942, *Meet Me in St. Louis* in 1944, *The Harvey Girls* in 1946, *The Pirate* and *Easter Parade*, both in 1948, and *Summer Stock* with Gene Kelly in 1950. With each, she added songs to her immortal repertoire.

The pictures she made were heaven, but Garland was going through hell in her private life. Although there was much joy, Garland was battling with alcohol and addiction. She did stints in rehab, had nervous breakdowns and numerous affairs, and attempted suicide more than once. Her off-screen trials and tribulations often made for more headlines than her fabulous work, which was just too bad. But her talent wouldn't be silenced. Garland's stage performances, like those at the Palace in 1951, became the stuff of legend.

Her brilliant turn as singer-turned-movie-star Esther Blodgett in the 1954

George Cukor remake of *A Star is Born*, opposite James Mason, garnered her tremendous acclaim. Although the Oscar went to Grace Kelly in *The Country Girl*, *A Star is Born* is considered some of Garland's best work. Her 1960s TV series *The Judy Garland Show* still has many fans thanks to DVD. Her final films—among them the historical drama *Judgment at Nuremberg* in 1961 and the musical *I Could Go on Singing* in 1963, starring Dirk Bogarde—live on as well.

Garland's untimely death at age forty-seven is said to have played a part in the Stonewall uprising, the 1969 Greenwich Village, New York, riot that signaled the start of the gay rights movement. While she remains an enormous favorite of gays—singer Rufus Wainwright performed her entire 1961 Carnegie Hall concert in the same venue in 2006; how's that for dedication?—it's important to remember that Garland was *everyone's* favorite during her lifetime. Drag artistes still make themselves up as Judy, but so do women. British actress Tracie Bennett received a 2012 Tony nomination for her portrayal of Garland on Broadway in the musical drama *End of the Rainbow*. Whatever your gender, you'll get raves when you cook Garland's ham casserole.

CHRISTMAS TIDBIT

Judy Garland's 1963 Christmas special—actually the December 22 episode of her weekly CBS series *The Judy Garland Show*—remains a perennial treat. Performed as if it were a holiday party in the Garland home, the show featured Judy's children, Liza Minnelli, Joey Luft, and Lorna Luft, not to mention the singers Mel Torme and Jack Jones. There's great music and a high camp factor. In 2011, *Glee* parodied the special in all its gayness, bringing the original's effervescence to a new generation while adding a same-sex duet of "Let It Snow." Both shows are available on DVD and make a scrummy double-feature.

CHRISTMAS IN TINSELTOWN

JUDY GaRLanD's Ham casserole WiTH SHerry

Preheat oven to 350 degrees. Combine the ham, rice, cream, eggs, tomatoes, pepper, onion, mustard, Worcestershire sauce, and sherry. Mix well and transfer to a greased two-quart casserole dish. Mix the bread crumbs, melted butter, and paprika, and sprinkle on top of the ham mixture. Bake 45 minutes.

4 cups ground cooked ham

2 cups cooked rice

½ cup heavy cream

2 eggs, well beaten

2 tomatoes, peeled and chopped

2 tablespoons diced green pepper

1 tablespoon grated onion

1 teaspoon prepared mustard

1 teaspoon Worcestershire sauce

½ cup sherry wine

¾ cup bread crumbs

1 tablespoon butter, melted

½ teaspoon paprika

Vincente Minnelli, 1903–1986

H IS FATHER WAS A MUSICIAN AND HIS MOTHER WAS AN ACTRESS, so maybe he had no choice but to go into show business. But that doesn't diminish Vincente Minnelli's meteoric rise from his hometown of Chicago to the bright lights of New York and Hollywood. The man went from working as a window dresser, to designing sets and costumes for Broadway, to directing such classic films as *An American in Paris* and *Gigi*. He made comedies and dramas, but Minnelli would become best known as, in the words of lyricist Alan Jay Lerner, "the greatest director of motion picture musicals the screen has ever known."

Summoned to Hollywood in 1940 by Metro-Goldwyn-Meyer mogul Alan Freed, Minnelli spent twenty-six years at that legendary studio. He turned out such well-regarded (if not always financially successful) films as *Cabin in the Sky* in 1943, *Meet Me in St. Louis* in 1944, *The Pirate* in 1948, *The Band Wagon* in 1953, and *Brigadoon* in 1954. His "serious" films included the 1952 melodrama *The Bad and the Beautiful* and the 1956 Vincent van Gogh biopic *Lust for Life,* both starring Kirk Douglas, and 1956's *Tea and Sympathy* with Deborah Kerr.

Minnelli counted among his leading ladies Elizabeth Taylor (in the 1950 comedy *Father of the Bride*), Lucille Ball (in 1953's *The Long, Long Trailer*), Lauren Bacall (in 1957's *Designing Woman*), and Barbra Streisand (in 1970's *On a Clear Day You Can See Forever*). But his greatest collaborator was Judy Garland. Minnelli's infatuation, film critics have noted, can be seen in the glowing ways in which he frames her on screen. During the years the two were married, from 1945 to 1951, he directed her in such films as *The Clock, Ziegfeld Follies*, and *The Pirate*.

Their greatest creation may have been Liza Minnelli, who was born to the couple in 1946. All three members of the family won the Oscar. Judy won one for her body of work as a juvenile actress in 1940. Vincente Minnelli got his for *Gigi* in 1958. Liza got hers for the 1972 musical *Cabaret*. The proud papa boasted in his 1974 autobiography *I Remember It Well*, "How many men can lay claim to being loved by the most extraordinary talents of not one, but two generations?"

Even so, it is believed that Minnelli struggled with his own conflicted sexuality—something discussed in detail in Mark Griffin's juicy 2010 biography, *A Hundred or More Hidden Things*—and that may have helped make him such an interesting and formidable filmmaker. Although some critics have dismissed his movies—Andrew Sarris once said, "Minnelli believes more in beauty than in art"—his body of work continues to delight audiences. Without the clips of Minnelli's movies, *That's Entertainment!* would have been called simply *That's*.

His chicken is something his films never were—simple. Enjoy.

vincente minnelli's chicken

Preheat oven to 425 degrees. Sprinkle salt and pepper inside the chicken. Stuff the cavity with the onions and the crushed sage leaves. Rub the outside of the chicken with olive oil. Sprinkle it with salt and pepper, the Italian herb blend, and the crushed garlic.

Cook the chicken, breast side up, for 15 minutes. While it's cooking, melt the butter and mix in the oil. After 15 minutes, reduce the oven temperature to 350 degrees and turn the chicken on its side. Cook for 15 minutes, basting with the butter-and-oil mixture. Turn the chicken onto its other side, and cook it for another 15 minutes, basting as before. Finally, turn the chicken breast side up and cook for another 35 minutes. Sprinkle with more salt and baste again.

Remove the cooked chicken from the oven, cover, and keep warm for 20 minutes. Thicken any pan drippings with a small amount of flour to make gravy.

Serves 2-4

1 (3–4 pound) chicken

Salt and pepper, to taste

2 large yellow onions, quartered

Fresh sage leaves, crushed

Olive oil

Italian herb blend

1 clove of garlic, crushed

4 tablespoons butter

4 tablespoons olive oil

Flour

6

MUNCH OF THE WOODEN SOLDIERS

efore the Old Woman Who Lived in a Shoe was Carrie Bradshaw on *Sex and the City*, back when Tom-Tom was the Piper's son and not a GPS device, there was *March of the Wooden Soldiers*.

The 1934 musical, starring Stan Laurel and Oliver Hardy and based on Victor Herbert's operetta *Babes in Toyland*, was broadcast every year between Thanksgiving and Christmas on WPIX in New York when I was a kid. They acquired the rights in the late 1950s and, as a *Village Voice* critic has noted, the film's annual airing became "nearly as significant a seasonal icon as Macy's Thanksgiving Day Parade or the tree at Rockefeller Center" for those of us who grew up in what our weatherman called "the tri-state area." It showed in other markets, too.

March is not technically a Christmas movie. It's set in July, for one thing. Santa Claus shows up twenty-five minutes in, complains that Laurel and Hardy have screwed up his toy order (like they need someone else bitching at them), and then he's gone. At one point, Ollie hides in a giant wrapped box marked DO NOT OPEN UNTIL CHRISTMAS, but that bit is over in a minute. And the wooden soldiers, who figure in the climactic battle scene, *were* supposed to be Christmas presents. The ligneous troops square off against Barnaby's Bogeymen, who look like Troll dolls in mohair onesies and little grass skirts.

Really, though, *March of the Wooden Soldiers* is a film about nursery-rhyme characters and the horrors befalling the old footwear-dwelling broad (Florence Roberts) and her daughter, Bo-Peep (Charlotte Henry), at the hands of the evil Silas Barnaby (Henry Brandon née Heinrich von Kleinbach). He holds a mortgage on the shoe and wants to marry Bo, even though he's too old for her and she's hot for Tom-Tom (Felix Knight) despite the fact that he's always wearing tights around town.

Every year we watched that damn movie. Revisiting it on Blu-ray as an adult, I'm struck by just how funny Laurel and Hardy are together, and how creepy Toyland is, with its three little rubber-faced pigs, its monkey in a Mickey Mouse costume throwing bricks at a giant man-cat, and its Old King Cole (Kewpie Morgan) who seems to think the death penalty is a laughing matter. The bloodthirsty blimp is ready to drown everyone, no matter how small the infraction. Honestly, Toyland is so weird it makes Munchkinland look like Levittown.

Laurel and Hardy, one of the rare acts able to successfully make the transition from silent films to talkies, were at the height of their fame when they took on the roles of Stannie Dee and Ollie Dum in *March*. (The film was known back then as *Babes in Toyland* and was not rechristened *March of the Wooden Soldiers* until a late 1940s theatrical rerelease.) A complete print of the film—the version many saw on TV had been cut for time—was believed to have been lost. After an international search and many false leads, a film historian found a pristine copy at Eastman House, the film repository in upstate New York.

In 1961, Disney remade the film as *Babes in Toyland* with a cast that included Annette Funicello, Ray Bolger, Tommy Sands, Tommy Kirk, and Ed Wynn. Ann Jillian, who went on to star in the hit '80s sitcom *It's a Living*, was Bo Peep. The original was colorized in the 1990s, which didn't downplay its weirdness any. But, thank heaven, it was restored in the original black-and-white, too.

March of the Wooden Soldiers may not be up there with such Laurel and Hardy classics as *Sons of the Desert* or *Way Out West*, but it's definitely worth watching at Christmastime. You've got to see it, if only to watch a heavily veiled Stan marry Barnaby (so Bo Peep won't have to) and then see him realize his gay marriage means he won't be living (and sharing a bed) with Ollie anymore. "I don't want to stay with him," Stan says to his roly-poly pal. "I don't love him."

Heck, maybe you should watch *March* in June instead.

STaN LaUreL, 1890–1965

ORN INTO AN ENGLISH THEATRICAL FAMILY, Stan Laurel was a pioneer in comedy even before he became the skinny half of the greatest comedy duo in film history. By the time he was twenty, Laurel was acting on stage alongside Charlie Chaplin, often as his understudy.

He went to America in the second decade of the 1900s; formed a variety act with vaudeville performer Mae Dahlberg, with whom he lived for years; and then made the leap to movies in the early 1920s. In 1927, Laurel and Hardy joined forces, and the rest, as they say, is hysterical.

Working first at the Hal Roach studio and later at 20th Century Fox, the duo made a slew of short films and such features as 1933's *Sons of the Desert,* 1934's *Babes in Toyland,* 1937's *Way Out West,* 1939's *The Flying Deuces,* and 1940's *A Chump at Oxford.* Their only real bomb was their last picture together, a 1951 French film called *Utopia.* Laurel's crying face and the words "Sorry, Ollie!" became part of pop culture. His protégé Dick Van Dyke did impressions for years.

When Hardy died in 1957, Laurel was said to have been inconsolable at the loss of his best friend and comic partner and suffered a nervous breakdown. He was much more upbeat about his own mortality, however. "If any of you cry at my funeral," he was quoted as saying, "I'll never speak to you again!" Before he died, Laurel received an Academy Award for lifetime achievement in film. On his deathbed, he was still the comedian. As the story goes, he told the nurse he wished he were skiing. She said she didn't know he was into that sport. "I'm not," Laurel replied, "but I'd rather be doing that than this."

His Ham Ring Mold should slide down easy.

STAN LAUREL'S HAM RING MOLD

Combine the soup and the water in a saucepan and heat. Beat the cream cheese in a bowl until smooth. Add the soup and mix well. Dissolve the gelatin in the water in another bowl. Add the gelatin to the soup-cheese mixture, mix until it's well combined, and refrigerate until partially set.

Combine the mayonnaise, mustard, lemon juice, and ground ham. Stir this ham mixture into the partially set soup-cheese mixture.

Oil a ring mold. Arrange the sliced egg and green olives on the bottom of the mold. Without disturbing the eggs and olives, pour in the gelatin mixture. Chill the mold until set. Unmold on a bed of lettuce and garnish with parsley.

1 can tomato soup

1 can water

1 (3 ounce) package of cream cheese

1¼ tablespoons unflavored gelatin

¼ cup water

½ cup mayonnaise

2 teaspoons prepared mustard

2 tablespoons lemon juice

2 cups ground cooked ham

2 eggs, sliced

4 stuffed green olives, sliced

Parsley for garnish

THE PLUMP, AMERICAN HALF OF Laurel and Hardy, Oliver Hardy began life as a Georgia boy with no interest in education and every desire to be in showbiz in any way he could. He took singing lessons as a kid, worked as a projectionist at a movie house near his hometown in his late teens, and shipped himself off to Florida, where some movies were being made, to be a film actor at twenty-one.

He made a slew of short films there and in New York before heading west in 1917. Later that year, he appeared in *The Lucky Dog*, a film which also featured Stan Laurel, although they were not yet a comedy duo and wouldn't be for years. Hardy alternated between playing the heavy and playing the comic relief. In 1925, he was the Tin Man in the silent version of *The Wizard of Oz* and was cast in the comedy short *Yes, Yes, Nanette*, which Laurel directed.

Two years later, Laurel and Hardy began in earnest as a comedy duo. Among their films—both short and feature length—were 1927's *The Battle of the Century*, 1929's *Unaccustomed as We Are* and *Berth Marks*, 1930's *Another Fine Mess*, and 1931's *Pardon Us*. Apart from Laurel—and with his blessing—Hardy appeared in the 1949 Western *The Fighting Kentuckian*, opposite John Wayne, and did a cameo in the 1950 Frank Capra comedy *Riding High*, with Bing Crosby.

A series of strokes ultimately did in the oversized funnyman at age sixty-five. Like Laurel, he smoked heavily, and he'd always been fat. Hardy didn't gain the extra poundage by eating the vaguely healthy recipe that he left behind, that's for sure.

I couldn't resist making that crack. Sorry, Ollie!

OLiver HardY'S Baked apples WITH Honey and almonds

Serves 4

4 baking apples

1 teaspoon aromatic bitters

4 tablespoons honey

4 tablespoons chopped blanched almonds

4 teaspoons butter

Whipped cream, for garnish

Preheat the oven to 375 degrees. Peel the top half of each apple. Remove the core of each without cutting through the bottom. Combine the bitters and the honey and put one tablespoon into each apple cavity. Brush the top and sides of the apples with the honey-and-bitters mixture. Put a tablespoon of chopped almonds in each cavity. Dot the top of each apple with a teaspoon of butter. Bake for 1 hour or until tender. Serve with whipped cream.

a christmas eve menu

If you think there's something fishy about eating meat on December 24, try this alternative—a meatless menu for a sumptuous Christmas Eve dinner.

starters

Thelma Ritter's Seafood Dip

Dean Martin's Baked Potatoes with Caviar

salad

Art Carney's Avocado-Grapefruit-Endive Salad

entrées

Reginald Denny's Broiled Lobster Tails

Boris Karloff's Halibut Royale

accompaniments

Charles Ruggles's Cauliflower and Mushroom Casserole

Elvis Presley's Hush Puppies

desserts

Donna Reed's Lemon Bundt Cake

Bing Crosby's Sugar Cookies

Spike Jones's Molasses Jumble Cookies

Norman Rockwell's Oatmeal Cookies

animation
MASTICATION

azzleberry dressing. Without the classic animated specials of the 1960s, we'd have none of it, and whatever it is, it must taste pretty good because that gimpy little Tiny Tim is *obsessed* with it in *Mr. Magoo's Christmas Carol*.

A 1962 musical version of the classic Charles Dickens short story, *Mr. Magoo's Christmas Carol* is one of the Big Three Christmas cartoons of the 1960s. No baby-boomer's holiday was ever complete without giving it an annual look-see along with those other two beloved specials, *A Charlie Brown Christmas* from 1965 and *Dr. Seuss's How the Grinch Stole Christmas!* from 1966. Even before the advent of home video, we had them memorized.

The truth is these programs are still more fun than almost all of the animated Christmas specials that came after them. I mean, I love *Shrek the Halls*, but it's no *Grinch*, even if the title characters *could* share the same foundation at the MAC counter.

Why do these oldies endure? Well, for one thing, they've got great songs. *Magoo* has "The Lord's Bright Blessing"—that razzleberry dressing song— and a score by Jule Styne and Bob Merrill, who went on to write the Broadway hit *Funny Girl*. *Charlie Brown* has "Christmastime Is Here" and a score by jazz great Vince Guaraldi. And who doesn't sing along with Thurl Ravenscroft as he sings "You're a Mean One, Mr. Grinch"? It's got lyrics by Seuss and music by Albert Hague, who wrote the '50s Broadway musicals *Plain and Fancy* and *Redhead*.

Another reason these three endure is that they manage to impart holiday wisdom in a way that's not heavy-handed. Despite the fact that Ebenezer/Magoo is blind as a bat and "too tight with a penny to buy a pair of spectacles," as the Ghost of Christmas Present tells him, he can see the future clearly enough to learn that unless he learns to share his wealth, he'll die miserable and alone, which would suck, especially on Christmas. The Peanuts

Backus as Magoo with a couple of *Christmas* turkeys.

gang learns that a crappy little sapling wrapped in a blanket beats a shiny aluminum tree any day. (I don't agree, but who am I to argue with Charles M. Schulz?) And the grouchy green one realizes that a heart "two sizes too small" should definitely be looked at by a doctor, preferably Seuss.

Mostly, though, these specials have genuine charm, a quality altogether lacking in contemporary society. They're gorgeous to look at and filled with as much cleverness as warmth. They're cute without being cloying. Watch them every year and, if you've got kids, introduce these specials to them. Their hearts will grow three sizes, too. But tell them to go easy on the raz-zleberry dressing or they won't have room for angel food cake with seven-minute frosting, a recipe for which you'll find in this chapter.

Jim Backus, 1913–1989

ALTHOUGH HE IS BEST KNOWN FOR playing the upper-crust cast-away Thurston Howell III on *Gilligan's Island* from 1964 to '67, Jim Backus was also the voice of Mr. Quincy Magoo, the nearly blind retiree who always manages to narrowly avoid the havoc he wreaks, in a series of cartoons beginning in 1949.

Backus had other regular TV roles over the years as well, including Judge Bradley Stevens on *I Married Joan* from 1952 to '55, and Mr. Dithers, Dagwood's boss, on a 1968 sitcom remake of *Blondie*. He was also the star of *The Jim Backus Show*, a very short-lived 1960 sitcom also known as *Hot Off the Wire*.

Backus appeared in some classic movies—1952's *Pat and Mike*, 1955's *Rebel Without a Cause,* and 1963's *It's a Mad, Mad, Mad, Mad World*—and also in such lovably bad '70s films as *Myra Breckenridge, Crazy Mama,* and *Friday Foster*. He was in the 1956 musical remake of *The Women* called *The Opposite Sex,* and the 1977 Disney picture *Pete's Dragon,* too.

For all he did, Backus is best remembered as the shipwrecked millionaire with a taste for the finer things in life. But every Christmas, those finer things are "razzleberry dressing" and "woofle jelly cake," served up by a repentant Scrooge who's as nearsighted as ever, but who learns to see the errors of his ways.

Here's Backus's tasty way with salad dressing. God bless us, everyone!

Jim Backus's Avocado Salad Dressing

Mash the avocado and transfer it and all of the other ingredients to a blender or food processor. Blend until thick. Serve immediately over any green salad.

Serves 10

1 avocado

¾ cup corn oil

⅓ cup lemon juice

1¾ ounces bleu cheese

1 clove garlic, minced

POST MORTEM

Be sure the avocado you use is perfectly ripe, or the taste and consistency of this dressing will suffer. To ripen a hard avocado, seal it in a brown paper bag. To speed the process, put a banana, an apple, or a tomato in there with it.

Boris Karloff, 1887–1969

BEST KNOWN FOR PLAYING THE MONSTER in *Frankenstein* and its two sequels in the 1930s, London-born actor Boris Karloff was synonymous with horror throughout his long career. Whether appearing opposite Bela Lugosi in such films as *The Black Cat* and *The Raven* in the 1930s, hosting the TV anthology series *Thriller* from 1960 to '62, or giving voice to the title character in *Dr. Seuss's How the Grinch Stole Christmas*, he was awfully sinister for someone born William Henry Pratt. And you should see him in drag as Mother Muffin on a 1966 installment of *The Girl from U.N.C.L.E.*—talk about scary!

Karloff began his acting career in Canada of all places. He began touring North America in various theatricals and then broke into silent films in the States, appearing in such early titles as 1920's *The Deadlier Sex*, 1922's *Omar the Tentmaker*—that's where that expression comes from!!!—and 1927's *Tarzan and the Golden Lion*.

His big break came in 1931 when James Whale cast him in *Frankenstein*. After his star turn in neck bolts, Karloff appeared in such well-regarded films as *Scarface, The Mask of Fu Manchu*, and *The Mummy*, all in 1932. He again played the monster in the classic 1935 sequel *Bride of Frankenstein*, and in 1939's not-so-hot *Son of Frankenstein*. Other noteworthy films include 1936's *Charlie Chan at the Opera*, considered to be one of the best *Chan* films, and *Isle of the Dead*, a 1945 cult favorite from director Val Lewton.

For the rest of his career, Karloff spent a lot of time living up to his name. He scared the wits out of Abbott and Costello in a couple of movies, played various mad scientists on *The Red Skelton Hour* over the years, played himself on a 1962 Halloween episode of *Route 66*, and, that same year, reprised

Mr. Grinch and Mr. Karloff.

his Broadway role in *Arsenic and Old Lace* in a TV version starring Tony Randall. In 1968, he lent his voice to the stop-motion animated classic *Mad Monster Party?* from producers Arthur Rankin and Jules Bass, whose work is discussed in Chapter 8. Once again, Karloff was a Frankenstein.

He made horror films right up until the end of his life. Four were released posthumously, proving you can't keep a good ghoul down. Here's his way with fish. Don't let the amount of butter scare you.

Boris Karloff's Halibut Royale

Preheat the oven to 450 degrees. In a sauté pan, lightly brown the onion rings in the butter. Transfer the onions to a shallow baking pan. Place the fillets on top of the onions. Beat the lemon juice and the egg yolks together. Bake the fish for 8 minutes, and then brush the fillets with the egg yolk–lemon mixture. Sprinkle the fillets with salt and paprika to taste. Return the fish to the oven and bake it for another 8 minutes. Do not overcook. To serve, mound the onions on a hot serving platter and place the halibut on top.

Serves 6

2 medium onions, sliced into rings

¼ cup butter

2 (1½ pound) halibut fillets

Salt, to taste

Paprika, to taste

2 tablespoons lemon juice

2 egg yolks

animation mastication

CHARLES M. SCHULZ, 1922–2000

HE IMAGINED A GREAT PUMPKIN soaring through the October sky, let a beagle become a World War I flying ace, named a bird Woodstock, and let a very bossy girl pull the football out from under his alter ego, a misfit boy named Charlie Brown, every time. Charles M. Schulz, the creator of the *Peanuts* cartoons, did as much to popularize the funny pages as anyone ever has.

An only child from Minneapolis who always liked to draw, Schulz returned home from a stint in the Army during World War II and, after working as an art teacher, launched a strip called *Li'l Folks* in the *St. Paul Pioneer Press*. It was a forerunner of *Peanuts*—one of the characters was even named Charlie Brown. Once Schulz sold *Peanuts* to United Features Syndicate in 1950, he was on his way to becoming the most adored American cartoonist in history.

Peanuts ran for almost half a century, at one point appearing in more than 2,600 newspapers in more than seventy-five countries. Characters from Linus to Peppermint Patty to the Little Red-Haired Girl were based on people that Schulz knew—and they reminded us very often of ourselves. That was always Schulz's strong suit. His characters may have had globes for heads, but they were us.

Today, his strips continue to be republished—Schulz stipulated that no *Peanuts* cartoons be drawn by anyone else—and his imagery continues to make tens of millions of dollars a year in licensing. Snoopy is as much a fixture in kids' lives today as he was forty years ago.

Although Schulz liked to say that the animated *Peanuts* specials were very much separate from the newspaper strip, they remain intertwined in our memories. Every December, *A Charlie Brown Christmas* is must-see

TV, a truly special special that reminds us of Schulz's brilliance. A museum dedicated to preserving his memory, the Charles M. Schulz Museum and Research Center, opened in Santa Rosa, California, several years after his death. One exhibit looked at food in the *Peanuts* comics. This recipe was said to be one of his favorites.

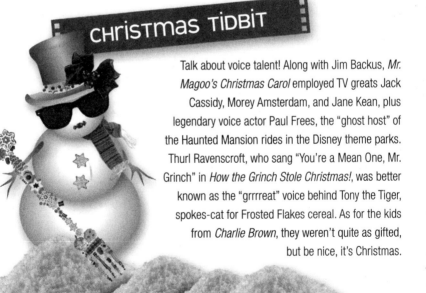

CHRISTMAS TIDBIT

Talk about voice talent! Along with Jim Backus, *Mr. Magoo's Christmas Carol* employed TV greats Jack Cassidy, Morey Amsterdam, and Jane Kean, plus legendary voice actor Paul Frees, the "ghost host" of the Haunted Mansion rides in the Disney theme parks. Thurl Ravenscroft, who sang "You're a Mean One, Mr. Grinch" in *How the Grinch Stole Christmas!*, was better known as the "grrrreat" voice behind Tony the Tiger, spokes-cat for Frosted Flakes cereal. As for the kids from *Charlie Brown*, they weren't quite as gifted, but be nice, it's Christmas.

CHarLes M. SCHULZ'S Favorite seven- Minute Frosting

Combine all of the ingredients in the top of a double boiler. Place the pan over boiling water and, with a hand-held electric mixer on high speed, beat the frosting for 7 minutes, or until peaks form when the beaters are lifted. Promptly use this icing to frost a store-bought angel food cake, or a homemade one like Joan Crawford's in Chapter 13.

2 egg whites

1½ cups sugar

5 tablespoons cold water

⅛ teaspoon salt

⅛ teaspoon cream of tartar

POST Mortem

Seven-minute frosting sounds easy, but getting it right isn't. Take care that the sugar completely dissolves or the frosting will be grainy, and don't plan on keeping it a long time. Your frosted cake will last at tip-top flavor only slightly longer than your dinner guests will.

RANKIN' THE NARRATORS

They called what they did "Animagic," and it was. In the 1960s and '70s, producers Arthur Rankin and Jules Bass took stop-motion animation and turned it into Christmas magic, and in so doing, cornered the market on seasonal specials.

They were the shizzle when it came to holiday TV.

Beginning in 1964 with *Rudolph the Red-Nosed Reindeer*—a Yuletide adventure about a fruity little dentist and a reindeer with self-esteem issues—Rankin/Bass produced such lovable programs as 1968's *The Little Drummer Boy*, 1970's *Santa Claus Is Comin' to Town*, and 1974's *The Year Without a Santa Claus*. That last one is the special that introduced the world to those evil, meteorological siblings, Snow Miser and Heat Miser, villains whose look, I'm convinced, inspired the men's hair on *Jersey Shore*.

There were other specials, like the 1969 charmer *Frosty the Snowman*, which they produced in traditional 2-D animation; a sequel to their original triumph called *Rudolph and Frosty's Christmas in July*; and various animated celebrations of Easter, too. A 1967 theatrical feature called *Mad Monster Party?*, starring puppet versions of Phyllis Diller and Boris Karloff (see Chapter 7), was Rankin/Bass's foray into Halloween territory and has major devotees—director Tim Burton among them—but that's for another book entirely.

The four big Rankin/Bass Christmas shows earned their bragging rights not only by looking adorable, but by sounding great. The scores—often by the very talented Maury Laws—were always top drawer, showcasing a popular Christmas song and then using it as a jumping-off place for a bevy of new tunes. Johnny Marks's work on *Rudolph* produced some of the greatest Christmas songs ever.

All the specials were voiced by stars drawn from Hollywood and Broadway, like Mickey Rooney, Jose Ferrer, June Foray, Keenan Wynn, George S. Irving,

Dick Shawn, and the incomparable Paul Frees. Over the years, Rankin/Bass also employed such venerable performers as Ethel Merman, Vincent Price, Jackie Vernon, Morey Amsterdam, and Shelley Winters.

Ives and his "Animagic" costars.

But what made the specials really special were the narrators. Each had a major celebrity—Burl Ives, Greer Garson, Fred Astaire, Jimmy Durante, Red Skelton, and Shirley Booth—rendered in animated form to lead viewers through the story. For many of us, these animated versions of the stars were our first exposure to them.

Mention Burl Ives and most of us instantly imagine a snowman in a vest. When we fell in love with him in 1964 we had no idea he'd played Big Daddy in *Cat on a Hot Tin Roof*. Jimmy Durante, to us, is the guy who waxed nostalgic about a puddle of slush named Frosty, not the big-nosed fella who sang "Inka Dinka Doo." Fred Astaire was a kindly mailman. Who knew he danced?

Although there have been big-budget sequels and remakes of classic Rankin/Bass properties in recent years, they've lacked the Animagic touch of the originals. A live-action TV remake of *The Year Without a Santa Claus* starring Delta Burke and John Goodman, for instance, was a notorious bomb in 2006. Carson Kressley as an elf stylist? Really?

Only 2001's *Santa, Baby!*, which Rankin executive produced, comes close to capturing the old formula. Gregory Hines and Eartha Kitt, whose recipe for Crocked Rabbit appears in Chapter 12, lend their voices, and none other than Patti Labelle narrates. It was, incidentally, the first Rankin/Bass special to feature a predominantly African American cast. If you can catch it on TV or DVD, do.

In the pages that follow, you'll find tributes to and recipes from those actors who narrated the best Rankin/Bass Christmas specials. They're gone, but their voices and images live on—and now their favorite foods can, too.

FreD asTaire, 1899–1987

I N THE YEARS BETWEEN HIS GOLDEN PERIOD in the mid-1930s—when he redefined "debonair" in such song-and-dance classics as *Top Hat* and *Swing Time*—and his golden years in the 1970s—when he played lovable con men in such films as *The Towering Inferno* and *The Amazing Dobermans*—screen legend Fred Astaire found time to narrate *Santa Claus Is Comin' to Town* in 1970.

If you were a child at the time, like I was, you had no idea that he was anyone but S. D. Kluger, the lovable mailman who told the tale of how Kris Kringle became Santa Claus.

Astaire, of course, was arguably the greatest hoofer to ever appear on film—inspiring filmmakers and dancers as disparate as Bob Fosse, Mikhail Baryshnikov, and Michael Jackson. Astaire entered show business via vaudeville as half of a brother-sister dance act with his older sibling, Adele. The reviews of their revues were often ecstatic. One paper called them "the greatest child act in vaudeville." As they matured, so did their dancing, until they became the toast of Broadway and the London theatre world.

When Adele got married, Astaire continued to perform—dazzlingly—and when audiences thought Fred couldn't get any better, he was paired with Ginger Rogers, and together they hit new heights. That legendary meeting came in 1933's *Flying Down to Rio*. The movie was a Dolores Del Rio vehicle, but Astaire and Rogers stole the picture. *Variety* called him "distinctly likeable" and said that as a dancer he was "in a class by himself." Together, Fred and Ginger transported Depression audiences to a world of grace and affluence in such pictures as *The Gay Divorcee, Roberta, Follow the Fleet,* and *Carefree.*

In the 1940s, Astaire made such pictures as *Holiday Inn* with Bing Crosby (see Chapter 3), *You'll Never Get Rich* with Rita Hayworth, *Yolanda and the Thief*, directed by Vincente Minnelli (see Chapter 5), and *Easter Parade* with Judy Garland (ditto). Entering his fifties didn't slow him down. He danced on the walls and ceiling in 1951's *Royal Wedding*; partnered with such long-stemmed lovelies as Leslie Caron in 1955's *Daddy Long Legs*, Audrey Hepburn in 1957's *Funny Face*, and later that year, Cyd Charisse in *Silk Stockings*; and he garnered rave reviews in a serious role in the 1959 nuclear holocaust drama *On the Beach*.

In the 1970s, thanks to the success of the *That's Entertainment* pictures, new audiences were exposed to clips of Astaire's greatest work—this was before YouTube, you have to remember—and were blown away. Yes, that guy who was a guest star on *Battlestar Galactica* in 1979 had been a dancer forty years earlier. At Christmas, though, Astaire is the one and only S. D. Kluger, and will be as long as *Santa Claus* keeps *Comin' to Town*. His chicken soup will take the chill off after a long day on the mail route.

CHRISTMAS TiDBiT

Other actors have narrated more than one Rankin/Bass Christmas special—Greer Garson voiced *The Little Drummer Boy* and its sequel, *The Little Drummer Boy Book II*—but Fred Astaire was the only celebrity narrator to celebrate two holidays in the same role. Seven years after *Santa Claus Is Comin' to Town*, Astaire appeared again as S. D. Kluger in *The Easter Bunny Is Comin' to Town*.

Fred Astaire's Chicken Soup with Homemade Noodles

Serves
6-8

To make the noodles, beat the salt into the eggs and then add the eggs to the flour. Mix thoroughly using a wooden spoon until a stiff dough has formed. Turn out onto a lightly floured board and knead until smooth and elastic. Roll out the dough to ⅛-inch thickness and leave to dry for 30 minutes. Using a sharp knife, cut the dough into strips. Leave the strips to dry completely, about an hour.

To make the soup, wash the chicken and cut it into serving pieces. Put the chicken into a large stockpot with the cold water and bring it to a boil. Simmer the chicken about 90 minutes. Add the remaining ingredients (except for the eggs and the ice water) and cook another 15 minutes. Strain the broth, reserving the chicken, and cool. Refrigerate the chicken stock and when cold, remove any chicken fat that forms on the top.

Reheat the broth. To clarify the broth, beat the eggs and add them to the broth with the shells. Stir the soup until it simmers, then boil it for 2 minutes. Add the ice water. Set aside for 10 minutes and then strain it through a double layer of cheesecloth. Reheat the broth again and add the noodles. Simmer until the noodles are cooked, about 10 minutes. Adjust the seasonings to taste and serve.

Noodles

½ teaspoon salt

2 eggs

2 cups all-purpose flour

Soup

1 (4–5 pound) chicken

4 quarts cold water

8 peppercorns

2 cloves

1 small yellow onion

1 tablespoon salt

6–8 sprigs parsley

2 stalks celery

2 bay leaves

2 eggs (with shells)

1 tablespoon ice water

Greer Garson, 1904–1996

I N THE 1930S AND EARLY '40S, she was known for such films as *Goodbye, Mr. Chips, Madame Curie, Pride and Prejudice, Random Harvest*, and the film that won her the Academy Award, *Mrs. Miniver*. But at Christmastime, Greer Garson is remembered most vividly as the overly dramatic woman who narrates the 1968 Rankin/Bass classic, *The Little Drummer Boy*. When that little lamb becomes the victim of a hit-and-run chariot accident, you could cry your eyes out!

Discovered in her native London by legendary studio chief Louis B. Mayer, Garson was nominated seven times for the Oscar. Five of the nominations were in a row! The late '40s and the '50s were less kind to her, but she rebounded when she played Eleanor Roosevelt in *Sunrise at Campobello* in 1960. She received her seventh Academy Award nomination for the role. Her other '60s hits included *The Singing Nun*, starring Debbie Reynolds, and the Disney movie *The Happiest Millionaire* opposite Fred MacMurray.

Garson appeared on *Father Knows Best* as herself, and also was featured in the 1978 TV movie version of *Little Women*, which starred three of TV's most popular actresses of the day—Meredith Baxter, Susan Dey, and Eve Plumb. My favorite thing about her is that when she narrated *The Little Drummer Boy*, she was billed as *Miss* Greer Garson. Here's her way with guacamole. It's no miss.

Greer Garson's Guacamole

Peel the tomato and the onion and finely chop them. Finely chop the hot pepper. Peel and dice the avocados. Combine the chopped vegetables and avocados in a mixing bowl.

Mix the oil, mayonnaise, lemon juice, salt, and Tabasco. Gently toss the avocado mixture with this dressing. Serve the guacamole on a bed of shredded lettuce with plenty of tortilla chips.

1 small tomato

1 small onion

1 small red hot pepper

6 avocados

1 teaspoon vegetable oil

2 tablespoons mayonnaise

2 teaspoons lemon juice

2½ teaspoons salt

4 drops Tabasco sauce

Shredded lettuce

Tortilla chips

POST MORTEM

Be sure to wear rubber gloves when you handle the hot pepper in this or any other recipe. If not, and you absentmindedly rub your eyes, you'll cry more than you did the first time you saw *Goodbye, Mr. Chips.*

Burl Ives, 1909–1995

BEFORE HE WAS SAM THE SNOWMAN who narrated the 1964 Christmas classic *Rudolph the Red-Nosed Reindeer*, Burl Ives was a traveling folksinger with a trunkful of hits including "The Blue-Tail Fly," and an actor who'd been in the Broadway cast of *Cat on a Hot Tin Roof* in the 1950s. He did the movie, too.

Born into an Illinois farm family, Ives got started in show business as an actor/singer who traversed the country collecting songs and performing. He recorded dozens of albums and was a top-selling folk artist. What you need to remember is that he was the Jimmy Crack Corn guy and don't say, "I don't care."

The troubadour made his first movie *Smoky*, in 1946. He was briefly blacklisted, but after testifying before the House Un-American Activities Committee, a move that cost him the friendship of fellow folksinger Pete Seeger, he went back to work—and work, he did. He made such noteworthy films as *East of Eden, Desire Under the Elms, The Big Country,* and *Our Man in Havana.*

Later, television kept him busy until he was almost 80. In the 1960s, he appeared on various variety shows and played Gepetto in a TV version of *Pinocchio.* In the '70s, he had recurring roles on such series as *Alias Smith and Jones* and *The Bold Ones: The Lawyers.* He had a part in the landmark 1977 miniseries *Roots;* narrated *The Ewok Adventure,* a *Star Wars*–inspired TV movie from 1984; and played F. W. Woolworth in 1987's *Poor Little Rich Girl: The Barbara Hutton Story* starring Farrah Fawcett.

But with all that he did, Ives will always be best remembered as a snowman. You'd think his recipe would be for Baked Alaska, but guess again.

BURL IVES'S
STUFFED LEG OF
GOAT HAWAIIAN

Have your butcher debone a leg of goat. Brush the outside with lemon juice. Prepare the stuffing by tossing together the garlic, onion, 2 tablespoons melted butter, parsley, ginger, and pineapple. Mix in the bread crumbs. Season with salt and pepper. Stuff the bone cavity and tie with kitchen string. Brush with the remaining 2 tablespoons melted butter. Sprinkle with ginger, salt, and pepper.

Preheat the oven to 425 degrees. Roast the stuffed leg of goat for 30 minutes, then reduce the heat to 275 degrees, and continue to cook for 2–2½ hours. Baste with pineapple juice every half hour. Remove from the oven, cover with foil, and let it rest for 15 minutes before carving.

1 (5-pound) leg of goat

Juice of one lemon

½ clove garlic, minced

1 tablespoon grated onion

4 tablespoons melted butter, divided

2 tablespoons finely chopped parsley

½ teaspoon ground ginger (plus more for sprinkling)

1 cup crushed pineapple

2 cups bread crumbs (preferably made from cinnamon bread)

Salt and pepper to taste

Pineapple juice for basting

HEY CALLED HIM "THE SCHNOZZ" because his protuberant proboscis was to normal noses what Dolly Parton's outsized cleavage is to the average bosom. But it was the charm behind that schnozzola, his winning way of putting across a song like "Inka Dinka Doo," "Make Someone Happy," "As Time Goes By," and especially "Frosty the Snowman," that made Jimmy Durante one of the all-time greats.

A singer, pianist, and actor, blessed with a gravelly voice and great comic timing, Durante got his start in vaudeville, then moved up to Broadway in such legendary shows as Billy Rose's *Jumbo* and *Red, Hot and Blue,* and then broke into movies. Durante's film career ran the gamut from the 1932 Buster Keaton picture *The Passionate Plumber* to the sidesplitting 1963 Stanley Kramer comedy *It's a Mad, Mad, Mad, Mad World.*

Many of us fell in love with him via television. He hosted various variety shows in the 1950s, including his own eponymous series from 1954 to 1956. He continued appearing on variety shows until he was past eighty. In one of his most memorable roles, Durante was Humpty Dumpty—dressed by Bob Mackie, no less!—in the 1966 special *Alice Through the Looking Glass.* (That, you might remember, was the one in which Jack Palance played a menacing Jabberwock and looked like he was going to the Black Party.) Durante was a good egg.

Durante's songs are heard on numerous soundtracks to films released well after his death, among them *City Slickers, Sleepless in Seattle,* and *The Notebook.* No one uses his many catchphrases—"I got a million of 'em," "Everybody wants to get into the act," and "Goodnight, Mrs. Calabash, wherever you are"—anymore. But at Christmastime, Durante and *Frosty the Snowman* are never far from our hearts, or televisions. Although he was Italian, the recipe he left behind is German. It's inka-dinka-delicious, too!

Jimmy Durante's German Cole Slaw

Finely shred the cabbage. Finely chop the onion. Mix the cabbage and the onion. Sprinkle the vinegar on top and season with salt and pepper.

Dice the bacon and fry it until crisp. Pour the bacon and the fat over the cabbage mixture. Toss until all the cabbage is coated. Serve at once.

Serves 6

1 medium head of cabbage

1 medium onion

¼ cup cider vinegar

Salt and pepper, to taste

5 slices bacon

SHiRLEY BOOTH, 1898–1992

HOW CAN ANYONE NOT LOVE SHIRLEY BOOTH?

Not only was she a "doozy" of a domestic on *Hazel* from 1961 to 1966, she was also Mrs. Santa in *The Year Without a Santa Claus* in 1974. And that's not the half of it! Booth had a theatrical career that lasted almost fifty years, and she is one of the very few actors to have won a Tony and an Oscar for the same role, as the devastatingly sad housewife in the rip-your-guts-out 1952 classic *Come Back, Little Sheba*. She also won two Emmys and two more Tony Awards, if you're counting, and previously had garnered acclaim for the radio hit *Duffy's Tavern*.

Although the role is better known from its musical interpretations by Carol Channing and Barbra Streisand, Booth played Dolly Gallagher Levi in the 1958 film *The Matchmaker*, based on the Thornton Wilder play that became the basis for *Hello, Dolly*. Her appearance as Amanda in a 1966 TV production of *The Glass Menagerie* was lauded, too. And it's worth noting that besides *Hazel*, Booth also did a second, albeit short-lived, sitcom, *A Touch of Grace*, in 1973, that costarred fellow oldster J. Pat O'Malley and was a forerunner of *The Golden Girls*.

It was on stage, though, that Booth really shone. A veteran of hundreds of theatrical productions, she starred in such shows as *The Philadelphia Story*, *My Sister Eileen*, *A Tree Grows in Brooklyn*, and *The Desk Set* and blew audiences away every time. Legendary playwright George Abbott said of all the actresses with whom he'd ever worked, "Shirley is easily tops." And as the esteemed *New York Times* critic Brooks Atkinson once wrote, "The stage begins to glow the moment she steps on it and the audience melts."

Booth's recipe for pumpkin bread will win you glowing reviews.

SHiRLeY BOOTH'S PumPKiN BReaD

Preheat the oven to 325 degrees. Sift the dry ingredients—except for the 1 tablespoon of flour—together in a large bowl. In another bowl, beat together the oil, eggs, water, and pumpkin. Blend in the dry ingredients. Toss the raisins or chopped dates with the remaining tablespoon of flour, add them to the mixture, and stir to combine. Spread the batter in a greased and floured loaf pan and smooth the top.

Bake for 1½ hours.

1⅔ cups, plus
  1 tablespoon flour

1 cup sugar

¼ teaspoon baking powder

1 teaspoon baking soda

¾ teaspoon salt

½ teaspoon ground cloves

½ teaspoon nutmeg

½ teaspoon cinnamon

½ cup vegetable oil

½ cup water

1 cup canned pumpkin

2 eggs

1 cup raisins or chopped dates

CHRiSTMaS TiDBiT

Shirley Booth celebrated the holidays with Christmas-themed episodes twice during the run of *Hazel*—first in 1961 and then again in 1964. In the season one episode "Hazel's Christmas Shopping," out on DVD, the merry maid takes a night job at a local department store to earn extra money for presents. While she's no one's idea of the perfect saleslady—one snooty customer (Eleanor Audley of *Green Acres*) reports her to management—Hazel inadvertently foils a shoplifter's plans to loot the place of everything from a typewriter to a television.

RED SKELTON, 1913–1997

I'T'S NOT COOL TO ADMIT THIS, but I love Red Skelton and I have since I was a baby and thought his name was Red Skeleton. Yes, he was corny in the '60s. Yes, he laughed at his own jokes. And, yes, he was both a mime (gasp) and a clown (double gasp) who painted clown portraits (triple gasp) and sold them for upward of $80,000 apiece (shut up!).

But he was also adorable.

Whether sticking his thumbs under his arms to play talking seagulls Gertrude and Heathcliffe, or kicking a grown-up in the shin as the ever-prankish "Mean Widdle Kid," or taking to the ring as the punch-drunk boxer Cauliflower McPugg, audiences couldn't get enough of his hilarity.

His characters, like the lovable hobo Freddie the Freeloader, were a staple of his long-running variety show, which lasted from the early 1950s to the early 1970s. When it was cancelled, he persisted and it paid off. In 1976, Skelton, in puppet form, starred as Father Time in *Rudolph's Shiny New Year*. It's his most frequently seen TV appearance these days.

Before television, Skelton was a radio and movie star who had appeared in such films as the 1942 Cole Porter musical *Panama Hattie*, 1943's *Du Barry Was a Lady* with Lucille Ball and Gene Kelly, and the 1945 revue *Ziegfeld Follies*. He also starred in a number of films with legendary swimmer Esther Williams, most notably 1949's *Neptune's Daughter*.

He always believed that the best comedy was squeaky clean, which didn't endear him to young audience members (except me) in the gritty 1970s. His *New York Times* obituary quotes Skelton as saying that he'd rather be called "hokey" than "dirty." He maintained, "I don't think anybody should have to pay money at the box office to hear what they can read on restroom walls."

After CBS cancelled his TV variety show, Skelton was devastated, but he took to the college circuit, as if to prove that one is never too old to clown and make audiences scream with laughter. That's when I saw him, and yes, he was corny and yes, he laughed at his own jokes and yes, I loved him. So did every other person in that college auditorium. When he ended the evening with his signature "Good night and God bless," we knew we'd seen one of the greats. Enjoy his lima bean recipe. His ham hock isn't so much hokey as smoky.

CHRISTMAS TIDBIT

Red Skelton's ties to Christmas include not only *Rudolph's Shiny New Year,* but also his final TV project, the 1982 TV movie *Freddie the Freeloader's Christmas Dinner.* It costars Imogene Coca (whose recipe for Beef Quixote appears in *The Dead Celebrity Cookbook*) and Vincent Price and is included in the DVD box set *The Red Skelton Collection.* Other Christmas-themed Skelton skits, including one costarring Greer Garson, are available on various other compilations.

RED SKELTON'S HAM HOCK AND LIMA BEANS

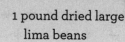

Place the lima beans in a pot with water to cover and allow to soak overnight. The next day, drain the beans, reserving the water, and place them in a stockpot. Add half of the reserved water. Cover and cook the beans over low heat for 15 minutes. Meanwhile, dice the onion, celery, and carrots. Add them to the pot along with the seasoning, and simmer for another 15 minutes. Wash the smoked ham hock and add it to the bean mixture. Simmer everything over low heat for 1 hour more, adding additional reserved water if needed.

1 pound dried large lima beans

1 smoked ham hock

1 large onion

2 large stalks of celery

2 large carrots

1 teaspoon salt

2 whole peppercorns

Pinch of nutmeg

POST MORTEM

Are you squeamish about cooking with ham hocks? (Sorry, Red, but they creep me out.) Instead, use a leftover ham bone with some meat left on it. Look in the freezer. There's probably one in there from *last* Christmas just itching to be rescued from the cold.

9

"Force" YOURSELF TO BE MERRY

It is perhaps the most notorious two hours in TV history—a Christmas special so cheesy, so what-the-hell-were-they-thinking? weird, so genuinely bad (and not *good* bad, either) that it makes *Ernest Saves Christmas* seem like *It's a Wonderful Life*. It is, of course, *The Star Wars Holiday Special*, the infamous 1978 TV extravaganza that George Lucas wishes he could blow up like the Death Star.

The Force was not with the now legendary writer-director the day he licensed his characters to Smith-Hemion Productions, a company that specialized in such television spectaculars as *At Home with Shields and Yarnell*. Along with Lucas's characters—Luke Skywalker, Han Solo, and Princess Leia—came the young actors who played them: Mark Hamill, Harrison Ford, and Carrie Fisher. Anthony Daniels in full C-3PO armor; Peter Mayhew covered in fur as Chewbacca; Alec Guinness, who was Obi Wan Kenobi; and James Earl Jones, as the voice of Darth Vader, participated, too.

The strange thing, though, was who *else* was in the special.

Somehow, comedy veterans Art Carney, Bea Arthur, and Harvey Korman were cast as various denizens of outer space. (Carney plays a trader. Arthur tends bar in a Tatooine cantina. Korman hosts an alien cooking show.) Diahann Carroll shows up, too, in holographic form. How completely bizarre is it to find the legendary actors who played Ed Norton, Maude Findlay, Mother Marcus, and Dominique Devereaux—not to mention members of the rock group Jefferson Starship—sucking out loud together in a galaxy far, far away.

Of course, *The Star Wars Holiday Special* was a long time ago, before the film upon which it was based had achieved the mammoth cultural significance it has today. The low-budget movie had been out only a year and a half at that point, and no one, except perhaps George Lucas, had any idea that *Star Wars* would spawn two sequels, three prequels, innumerable parodies

Korman and Arthur in a galaxy far, far away.

from *Saturday Night Live* to *Family Guy*, and a merchandising juggernaut, and shape the consciousness of generations to come.

In the special, which has never been rebroadcast and circulates only on bootleg DVDs, Chewbacca and Han Solo are heading to Kashyyyk to celebrate Life Day (Wookiee Christmas, essentially) with Chewie's family. It's a deranged mix of outer space intrigue, variety show shenanigans, a cartoon, and songs from Bea Arthur and Carrie Fisher. You really do have to see it. Once.

Daniels has called *The Star Wars Holiday Special* "horrible." Lucas has been quoted as saying "If I had the time and a sledgehammer, I would track down every copy of that show and smash it." The show's greatest distinction, though, came from a 2004 book about embarrassing television which ranked it—lock, stock, and Boba Fett—as the dumbest event in TV history. In a *New York Times* article a couple of years ago, though, Fisher looked on the bright side, and even admitted that she likes to show the special at parties. "Mainly at the end of the night," she said, "when I want people to leave."

You, however, might get your guests to stay all night with tasty recipes like these from four dearly departed members of the special's cast.

Bea Arthur, 1922–2009

W HEN SHE WASN'T TENDING BAR IN AN alien-filled Tatooine cantina on *The Star Wars Holiday Special*, actress Bea Arthur was endearing herself to generations of TV viewers, first as the uber-liberal Maude Findlay on *Maude* from 1972 to 1978, then as Dorothy Petrillo Zbornak Hollingsworth, the sharp-tongued but softhearted schoolteacher on *The Golden Girls* for seven seasons beginning in 1985.

Theatre lovers were already familiar with her deep voice and slow burn, most notably from Arthur's Tony Award–winning performance as Vera Charles, the boozy bosom buddy in Jerry Herman's 1966 Broadway musical *Mame*. (Arthur did the 1974 film version starring Lucille Ball, too, and was the best thing about it.) Her other important stage roles were Lucy Brown in a landmark 1954 production of *The Threepenny Opera* and Yente in *Fiddler on the Roof* in 1964.

Although she'd never intended to become a TV star, Arthur made such an impression as a guest star on *All in the Family* in 1971, playing Edith Bunker's cousin Maude, that there was no turning back. Her oft-repeated *Maude* line, "God'll get you for that!" became a catchphrase in the 1970s. And no one ever sang "Hold Tight" while smashing Andrews Sisters records with more hilarious determination. Fododo-de-yacka-saki indeed!

Over the years, the New York City native appeared on a short-lived Americanized version of the Brit hit *Fawlty Towers* called *Amanda's* in 1983, guest-starred as an elderly babysitter on a 2000 episode of *Malcolm in the Middle*, played Larry David's mother on *Curb Your Enthusiasm* in 2005, and performed a profane reading of Pamela Anderson's memoirs on a roast of the *Baywatch* bombshell on Comedy Central that year, too. That was genius.

Arthur also had a very funny turn in the 1970 film comedy *Lovers and Other Strangers,* and a cameo in Mel Brooks's 1981 *History of the World, Part I,* too. For a real thrill, check out clips from her 1980 variety program, *The Beatrice Arthur Special,* on YouTube. She and Rock Hudson sing "Everybody Today Is Turning On" from the Broadway musical *I Love My Wife.* Drug humor set to music. Yay!

Over the years, the beloved actress nabbed two Emmy Awards, became a vegetarian and an animal rights activist, performed in a lauded one-woman show on Broadway, and, upon her death, donated hundreds of thousands of dollars to provide shelter for homeless gay kids. They, like everyone who tunes into daily reruns of *Golden Girls,* were moved to say, "Thank you for being a friend."

Bea arthur's avocados with Jellied consommé

Blend the consommé, sherry, and lemon juice and chill until set. Combine the sour cream and herbs. To assemble, halve the unpeeled avocados and remove the pits. Using a fork, flake the consommé mixture and then spoon it into the avocado halves. Top each with a dollop of the herbed sour cream. Serve immediately.

Serves 8

4 unpeeled avocados

1 (10½ ounce) can consommé (with gelatin added)

2 tablespoons sherry

1 tablespoon fresh lemon juice

1 cup sour cream

1 tablespoon chopped chives, dill, or parsley

arT carneY, 1918–2003

e may have played Trader Saun Dann, a Rebel Alliance member who helps Chewbacca, on *The Star Wars Holiday Special*, but that certainly wasn't Art Carney's first foray into Christmas programming. The consummate character actor memorably starred as a drunken department store Santa in the 1960 *Twilight Zone* episode "Night of the Meek," and as the real Santa in the 1970 TV movie *The Great Santa Claus Switch* and again in 1984's *The Night They Saved Christmas*. (June Lockhart of *Lost in Space* played his missus in that last one.)

Pretty impressive for a skinny guy!

Starting as a comic singer on 1930s and '40s radio, Carney moved into television when that medium surged in the '50s. He turned up over the years on everything from *The Martha Raye Show* to *What's My Line?* I always remember him as the evil Archer on *Batman* in 1966. On stage, he triumphed as the original Felix Ungar, opposite Walter Matthau (and later Jack Klugman), in Neil Simon's *The Odd Couple* from 1965 to '67. (They didn't spell it "Unger" until it got to TV.)

In the 1970s, Carney turned to film and won the Academy Award for his starring role in 1974's *Harry and Tonto*, about an old coot and his cat. Other roles included an aging detective in 1977's *The Late Show* with Lily Tomlin, a bored retiree who takes to robbing banks in 1979's *Going in Style* with George Burns, and smallish parts in 1984's *The Muppets Take Manhattan* and 1993's *Last Action Hero*, starring Arnold Schwarzenegger, which was Carney's final film role.

No matter what else Carney did in his long career, though, he will forever be remembered as Ed Norton, the rubber-limbed friend and neighbor to corpulent bus driver Ralph Kramden (Jackie Gleason) on *The Honeymooners* beginning in the 1950s and continuing through the 1970s. Whether he was warming up on the piano by repeatedly playing the same few bars of "Swanee River," or, with club in hand, addressing a golf ball by saying "Hello, ball!" Norton was as funny a sewer worker as America has ever seen.

It wasn't always easy being so identified with that role, however. As Carney said in a 1974 interview, "How would *you* like to go through life with your name synonymous with sewage?" Now that you have his Avocado, Grapefruit, and Endive Salad recipe in hand, you'll think of him in a considerably more delicious way.

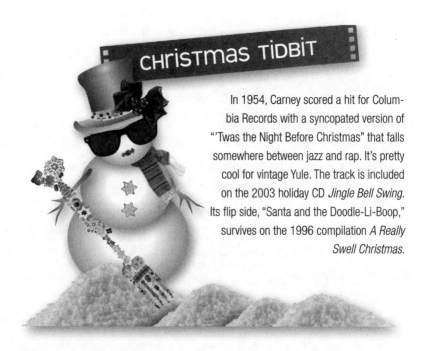

CHRISTMAS TIDBIT

In 1954, Carney scored a hit for Columbia Records with a syncopated version of "'Twas the Night Before Christmas" that falls somewhere between jazz and rap. It's pretty cool for vintage Yule. The track is included on the 2003 holiday CD *Jingle Bell Swing*. Its flip side, "Santa and the Doodle-Li-Boop," survives on the 1996 compilation *A Really Swell Christmas*.

art carney's avocado, grapefruit, and endive salad

Peel and section the grapefruits. Peel the avocados, cut them into chunks, and squeeze lemon juice over them. Separate the endive leaves, rinse, and dry them well, preferably using a salad spinner.

To make the dressing, blend the vegetable oil little by little into the sour cream. Add the vinegar and seasonings and mix thoroughly.

To serve, arrange the grapefruit, avocado, and endive in a salad bowl. Pour the dressing over it. Sprinkle the salad with dill and serve promptly.

Serves 2-4

Salad

2 grapefruits

2 avocados

1 lemon wedge

2 endives

Fresh dill

Dressing

½ cup vegetable oil

3 tablespoons sour cream

1 tablespoon wine vinegar

Salt and pepper, to taste

aLec Guinness. 1914–2000

E STARRED IN HALF A DOZEN DAVID LEAN epics—among them 1957's *The Bridge on the River Kwai,* for which he won the Oscar, and the 1960s classics *Lawrence of Arabia* and *Dr. Zhivago.* But to anyone who grew up in the '70s, Alec Guinness is Obi-Wan Kenobi in *Star Wars.* The actor, who always seemed more Old Globe than Old Republic, even in outer space, played the role of the powerful Jedi in the first three *Star Wars* films. (Ewan McGregor took over in the prequels.)

Born in London, Guinness first came to prominence in John Gielgud's 1936 production of Hamlet. Three years later, he adapted the Dickens classic *Great Expectations* for the stage and appeared as Herbert Pocket. It was a role he'd go on to play in Lean's 1946 film version. After that big screen hit, Guinness delighted audiences playing eight different characters in 1949's *Kind Hearts and Coronets,* and appeared in 1948's *Oliver Twist* and 1951's *The Lavender Hill Mob.*

He went on to impersonate Pope Innocent III in the 1972 Franco Zeffirelli film *Brother Sun, Sister Moon,* and was a not-so-innocent Adolf Hitler in the 1973 biopic *Hitler: The Last Ten Days.* Guinness also played the blind butler in the 1976 Neil Simon detective spoof, *Murder by Death.* See it, even if he couldn't.

Guinness's greatest TV triumph came when he played espionage agent George Smiley in the British miniseries *Tinker Tailor Soldier Spy* in 1979 and its 1982 follow-up *Smiley's People.* Nothing, though, could take any of the light away from his turn in *Star Wars.* Even if he called the movies "fairy tale rubbish," Obi-Wan is the role for which he'll always be known. It should be mentioned that Sir Alec's TV résumé is technically unblemished by *The Star Wars Holiday Special.* He appears in it only via film clips. Here's his Force-ful way with baked peaches.

CHRISTMAS IN TINSELTOWN

aLec Guinness's Baked Stuffed Peaches

6 large, ripe peaches

4 almond macaroon cookies

1 tablespoon sugar

2 tablespoons butter, softened

Preheat oven to 350 degrees. Halve and pit the peaches. Crush the cookies and mix the crumbs with the sugar and butter. Fill the cavity of each peach half and place them in a shallow baking dish. Pour a little warm water in the pan to prevent sticking. Bake the peaches for 20 minutes. Serve warm.

CHrisTmas TiDBiT

Alec Guinness played Jacob Marley's ghost in *Scrooge*, Ronald Neame's 1970 musical version of *A Christmas Carol* starring Albert Finney, but it was no happy experience. As the story goes, Guinness suffered a double hernia flying around on a guy wire, and then, adding insult to that injury, his big musical number "Make the Most of This Life" was cut from the film.

"Force" YourseLF To Be Merry

Harvey Korman, 1927–2008

S ONE OF MEL BROOKS'S TROUPE, HARVEY KORMAN played the land-snatching attorney general Hedy, er, Hedley Lamarr in *Blazing Saddles* in 1974, the bondage-and-discipline–loving Dr. Charles Montague in *High Anxiety* in 1977, and the frequently mispronounced royal advisor Count de Monet in *History of the World, Part I* in 1981. He was in 1995's *Dracula: Dead and Loving It*, too, but let's not go into that. (It mostly sucked.)

But for all intents and purposes, the lanky comedian will always be known as the man that Tim Conway most liked to crack up on *The Carol Burnett Show*. And crack up, Korman did. The good-natured actor sometimes laughed at the pint-sized Conway's antics harder than the audience did, which made the classic variety show even more fun. It was must-see TV every week from 1967 to 1978.

Korman appeared in more than 250 episodes of *The Carol Burnett Show* and memorably created such characters as Rat Butler in the classic "Went with the Wind" spoof, Ed Higgins on the recurring "Family" skits, and Mother Marcus, the bosomy Yiddish grandmother that he based on his own. He garnered four Emmy Awards and a Golden Globe over his ten seasons with the show. He played Ed again on *Mama's Family*, the spin-off sitcom starring Vicki Lawrence.

Korman first studied drama in his native Chicago, then moved east and, for more than a decade, tried to break into the New York theatre world. "I tried to get on Broadway, on off-Broadway, under or beside Broadway," Korman said.

When that didn't pan out, he moved back to Chicago and then decided to give California a try. Needless to say, he was more successful breaking into television. Early in his career, he appeared on *The Danny Kaye Show*, provided the voice for the Great Gazoo on *The Flintstones*, and did multiple guest shots on series like *The Jack Benny Program, The Lucy Show,* and *The Munsters.* When he was cast on *The Carol Burnett Show*, his place in TV history was sealed. Even appearing on *The Star Wars Holiday Special* couldn't tarnish his reputation.

Late in his life, after making guest appearances on numerous shows (and having tried in vain to head up his own series), Korman reunited with Conway and toured America doing their classic routines and showing clips. It was a hit. Somewhere he's still laughing, I'm sure. His chicken stew will make you smile.

CHRISTMAS TIDBIT

The Star Wars Holiday Special isn't Harvey Korman's only Christmas one-off. *The Carol Burnett Show* regular also appeared in 1977's *The Carpenters at Christmas* (alongside Kristy McNichol) and in 1978's *The John Davidson Christmas Show* (with Linda Lavin), not to mention the 1996 Arnold Schwarzenegger holiday movie, *Jingle All the Way.* None come close to *The Star Wars Holiday Special* in sheer awfulness, but each tries!

Harvey Korman's Chicken Stew

Rinse and dry the chicken parts. Season them with salt and pepper and half of the garlic. Heat the margarine and the oil in a Dutch oven or stock-pot. Brown the chicken and remove. Pour off excess oil. Put the onion, leek, celery, and garlic in the pot and add the chicken broth. Bring to a boil. Return the chicken to the pot, cover it, and simmer for 30 minutes. Next, add the celery root, carrots, onions, potatoes, and mushrooms. Bring the mixture to a boil once again, and then simmer it until the vegetables are tender, about 25 minutes. Season the stew with salt and pepper. Ladle into large soup bowls and serve piping hot.

Serves 4-8

8 pieces of chicken (breasts and thighs)

Salt and pepper, to taste

3 cloves of garlic, chopped

3 tablespoons margarine

3 tablespoons vegetable oil

2 onions, chopped

2 leeks (white part only), chopped

1 stalk celery, chopped

3 cups chicken broth

1 celery root, peeled and cut into cubes

4 carrots, sliced

12 small white boiling onions

6 small potatoes, peeled and halved

½ pound small mushrooms

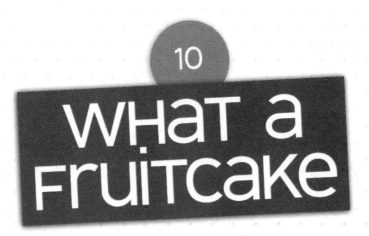

10

WHAT a Fruitcake

ther TV fanatics may have their own ideas about which Christmas spectacular is best. But I can't haul out the holly every year until I've watched the *Pee-wee's Playhouse Christmas Special*. No other TV celebration comes close to the sheer joy of this hour of seasonal song and small-screen silliness. It just isn't Christmas until that zany man-child in the too-tight plaid suit opens the padded red door to his playhouse and invites a world of cockamamie celebrities inside for a holiday party to end all holiday parties.

Originally broadcast in primetime on CBS in 1988, two Emmy-lavished years into the five-year run of *Pee-wee's Playhouse* on Saturday mornings, the *Pee-wee's Playhouse Christmas Special* is packed with talent. What other TV bash can boast a guest list that runs the gamut from Annette Funicello to Zsa Zsa Gabor?

There's k. d. lang in Patsy Cline overdrive, Cher looking as glittery as ever, Little Richard sweating up a storm, and Grace Jones delivered in an enormous box that was mailed to the White House but mistakenly ends up at the playhouse. No one has ever pa-rum-pa-pum-pummed her way through "The Little Drummer Boy" with more fashion chic than amazing Grace does in her Amazon chest plate and matching hat. Dinah Shore sings the world's longest version of *The 12 Days of Christmas*, and the Del Rubio Triplets, a trio of geriatric guitarists, strum their way through a winter wonderland while wearing hot pants.

I never saw any of the King Family grandparents do that!

William Marshall, who was the star of *Blacula* before he became the King of Cartoons on *Playhouse*, is along for the ride, as is Laurence Fishburne, who made his first big TV splash as Cowboy Curtis, and S. Epatha Merkerson, who was Reba the mail lady before she was Lieutenant Anita Van Buren on *Law & Order*. With them are special guests Joan Rivers, Oprah Winfrey,

Magic Johnson, Frankie Avalon, Whoopi Goldberg, and even Charo. The Spanish songstress's flamenco rendition of "Feliz Navidad" is *muy bueno*.

Written by Paul Reubens, who took his beloved Pee-wee character to Broadway in 2010, and John Paragon, known onscreen as the flamboyant genie Jambi, *Pee-wee's Playhouse Christmas Special* also includes a Hanukah number, introduced by Mrs. Rene (Suzanne Kent) to the delight of the miniature dinosaur family who lives in the playhouse. They're Jewish. Who knew?

This gloriously inclusive special lives on via DVD as the most memorable—if not the best—episode of a classic TV series that warped a generation of young minds. Opening with a choir of hunky Marines in full dress and closing with Pee-wee taking a ride in Santa's sleigh, it is as nutty as a fruitcake (I know you are, but what am I?) and twice as delicious. Be sure to savor it every year.

DiNaH SHore, 1916–1994

IN A CAREER THAT SPANNED more than half a century, singer, actress, and cookbook author Dinah Shore personified warmth and southern hospitality. Punctuating everything she did with a giant "mwah" of a kiss, Shore first made it big as a solo artist during the Big Band era with a string of chart hits like "Buttons and Bows" and "I'll Walk Alone." In the 1950s and '60s, she starred in her own eponymous TV variety shows.

This was before she established herself as a chummy chat show hostess who made everyone from Charles Nelson Reilly to Iggy Pop feel comfortable on her couch. If you grew up watching *Dinah!* in the '70s as I did, you know that nobody ever looked better in a maxi-skirt, either. No wonder her considerably younger suitor Burt Reynolds loved her for all those years!

In 1976, Shore made two of the most memorable guest appearances in TV history. She portrayed Melody, a saccharine-sweet take on Olivia de Havilland's role in *Gone with the Wind*, in the classic "Went with the Wind" spoof on *The Carol Burnett Show*. And Shore, who was Jewish, played herself in an episode of *Mary Hartman, Mary Hartman* that took on anti-Semitism in a hilarious fashion. In a show-within-a-show episode, country singer Loretta Haggers (Mary Kay Place) appears with Shore on live television and marvels that the Jews on Dinah's staff are so nice considering they are the people "what killed our lord."

It's a jaw-dropper.

A genuine gourmet in real life, Shore wrote a number of cookbooks, including 1971's *Someone's in the Kitchen with Dinah*. They pop up frequently at flea markets and are definitely worth adding to your kitchen library. Recently, Shore's name has become synonymous with an all-girl weekend held each year in Palm Springs, California. (Although the event is called "The Dinah," Shore probably wasn't a lesbian. But she *did* like to play golf.) A splashy tribute to the lovely lady came in 2011 when the cast of *Glee* re-created one of her vintage Chevy commercials, singing "See the U.S.A. in Your Chevrolet" in a TV spot that aired during the Super Bowl. Whether they knew it or not, millions of football lovers got a glimpse of the old Shore spirit. It was a kiss from a very special lady.

Her fruitcake, which should be made well before Christmas, will please your lips just as much as it did hers.

DINAH SHORE'S FRUITCAKE

Line 6 loaf pans with waxed paper, leaving extra paper above the rims. Preheat the oven to 300 degrees.

Mix the figs and dates with 1 cup of flour and set aside. Mix the remaining flour with the baking soda and the spices in a large bowl. In an even larger bowl, cream the butter, then add the sugar and egg yolks and beat well. Add the flour-spice mixture to the butter-egg mixture alternately with the molasses and the brandy. Stir in the dried fruit and nuts and mix well to evenly distribute them.

Divide the batter between the pans, making sure they're no more than ⅔ full. Place 3 loaf pans inside each of 2 roasting pans. Pour hot water into the roasting pans to a depth of 1 inch. Bake the fruitcakes 2½ hours, covering them with more waxed paper if they look too brown. Carefully remove the loaf pans from the water, and then bake the cakes without the water bath for half an hour more.

Remove cakes from the oven and let them cool for 10 minutes; turn them out of the pans, remove the waxed paper, and place the fruitcakes on a rack to cool completely. When they're cool, wrap them in fresh waxed paper and then aluminum foil. To keep the cakes fresh, sprinkle them with a little brandy every week until Christmas. They can be stored in a cool dry place for up to six months.

POST MORTEM

Dinah's original recipe mixes the dates, figs, and raisins into the batter, and then alternates layers of this batter with the remaining fruits and nuts. It's easier to just mix in all the ingredients, as above. Providing you're careful to evenly distribute the ingredients when you fill the loaf pans, the results will be just as toothsome.

1 pound dried figs, halved lengthwise, stems removed

1 pound pitted dates, halved lengthwise

4 cups flour, divided

1 teaspoon baking soda

1 teaspoon nutmeg

1 teaspoon cloves

2 teaspoons cinnamon

2 cups butter, softened

2 cups brown sugar

12 egg yolks

½ cup molasses

½ cup brandy

12 egg whites, beaten until firm but not dry

¼ pound candied orange rind, diced

¼ pound candied lemon rind, diced

1 pound golden raisins

1 pound seedless raisins

1 pound candied pineapple, diced

¼ pound citron

1 pound candied cherries

½ pound blanched almonds

½ pound pecans

½ pound English walnuts

11

a CHRISTMAS HOMECOMING

As squeaky-clean families go, they made the Bradys look like the Bundys.

But in December 1971, TV audiences fell in love with a humble Virginia clan named the Waltons on a holiday special called *The Homecoming: A Christmas Story*, starring Patricia Neal. Theirs was a homespun tale of life on Walton's Mountain during the Great Depression, as seen through the sharp eye and sensitive heart of a young writer named John-Boy.

He was the alter ego of series creator Earl Hamner Jr., who'd grown up in Schuyler, Virginia, in the Blue Ridge Mountains. Richard Thomas, an adorable actor whom I think of as the original celebrity mole, was a Manhattan-raised city kid—but you wouldn't know that from *The Waltons*. Thomas *was* John-Boy, and, even in his sixties, he still is that pillar of quiet fortitude and decency in many people's minds. He's still way cute, too.

Although *The Homecoming* wasn't intended as a pilot, audience response to the Waltons—all seven kids, two grandparents, and Ma and Pa—was so positive that CBS realized TV was ready for a weekly dose of retro-escapism.

When the show appeared the following fall, Neal was gone, replaced by Michael Learned as a somewhat less heavyhearted Olivia. (Honestly, Neal could be a downer.) Ralph Waite was the new John Walton. No one minded that change. The original actor who played him, Andrew Duggan, showed up only at the end of *The Homecoming*, anyway. The playful Will Geer—a bisexual communist, no kidding—took over for Edgar Bergen as Grandpa Zebulon Walton.

Needless to say, the series became a hit. For audiences, it was an hour of hope each week. If the Waltons could survive the Great Depression—not to mention Livvy's bout with polio and Grandma's stroke (written into the series after actress Ellen Corby had one in real life)—with love and dignity, America could survive the '70s. As Jon Walmsley, who played Jason

Thomas and Neal on Walton's Mountain.

Walton, has said, "The show wasn't just a show to some people. It had a deeper meaning."

Each episode of *The Waltons* ended with the family switching off their bedroom lights as they bid each other goodnight. It was a corny bit of business to be sure, but it became a pop culture touchstone. (If you watched the show as a kid, surely you've shouted out "Good night, John-Boy" in the dark at least once.)

Likewise the show's theme song, written by Jerry Goldsmith, still conjures up wholesome memories. Affection for it runs so deep that forty years after the show's premiere, Kellogg's used the music to underscore a commercial for a cereal called Fruit Harvest. In 2011, a cast reunion and screening of *The Homecoming* to celebrate the special's 40th anniversary drew more than a thousand Waltons worshippers to the Landmark Loew's Jersey Theatre in Jersey City, New Jersey. Not only did the special still pack an emotional wallop, but Richard Thomas did a dramatic reading of *The Night Before Christmas*. It really was quite an evening.

The Waltons, which ran until 1981, and then spawned a half-dozen TV movies that ran into the 1990s, wasn't the first time Hamner saw his life on screen. His novel *Spencer's Mountain*, which was the basis for the series, previously had been turned into a 1963 movie starring Henry Fonda. But a family named Spencer and a son named Clay-Boy? It doesn't stand up to *The Waltons*.

No one could have predicted when *The Homecoming* first aired that audiences would still toast it all these years later. But, like the bootlegging Baldwin Sisters, we do. If they'd shared "Papa's Recipe," as the Baldwins' moonshine was called, I would certainly have included it here. Instead, you'll find Bergen's Swedish meatballs and Neal's recipe for a dessert called Sunshine Parfait. Note to diehard *Waltons* fans: Geer's recipe for Walton's Mountain Muffins and Corby's for Apple Cake appear in *The Dead Celebrity Cookbook*.

VENTRILOQUIST EDGAR BERGEN—father of Candice—was "discovered" by Hollywood after doing his thing at an Elsa Maxwell party for Noel Coward, and then taking his act to New York's famed Rainbow Room. Talk about glamour!

A former vaudevillian, Bergen and his wooden sidekicks went on to a career in radio, appearing on Rudy Vallee's popular program and then *The Chase and Sanborn Hour*. The fact that it was radio ventriloquism didn't stop audiences from making Bergen one of the most beloved performers in America.

After doing a series of short films, Bergen won an honorary wooden 1938 Oscar for creating Charlie McCarthy. The following year, he appeared in the W. C. Fields film *You Can't Cheat an Honest Man*. Although Bergen moved his lips—a fact lampooned by McCarthy and pal Mortimer Snerd—he was a hit there, too.

As an actor, Bergen did a couple of movies with radio stars Fibber McGee and Molly, narrated the *Mickey and the Beanstalk* segment of the animated 1947 Disney movie *Fun and Fancy Free*, and appeared in 1948's *I Remember Mama* as a shy Norwegian suitor. Bergen, who was Swedish, was not quite as shy in real life. He spotted his future wife, eighteen years his junior, in the front row of one of his radio shows and asked that she be brought back to meet him afterward.

On television in the 1950s, Bergen hosted *The Colgate Comedy Hour* and appeared on numerous variety shows. In the 1960s and '70s, he guest-starred on everything from *What's My Line?* to *Laugh-In* to *The Brady Bunch Variety Show*. And, of course, he brought his talents to *The Homecoming* in 1971.

Bergen's appearance on *The Muppet Show* in 1977 led to a cameo in 1979's *The Muppet Movie*, which was released posthumously and dedicated to his memory.

At the height of Bergen's career, his most famous creation, Charlie McCarthy, had his own bedroom. Today the dummy resides, quite appropriately, at the Smithsonian Institution. Bergen was commemorated on a stamp. And daughter Candice paid tribute—of sorts—to him in her memoir, *Knock Wood*.

Here's his way with Swedish meatballs.

edgar bergen's swedish meatballs

Mix all of the ingredients except butter in a large bowl. Shape the meat mixture into 1-inch balls. Melt the butter in a sauté pan and fry the meatballs until brown and cooked through.

Serves 6

1 pound ground round

2 tablespoons minced onion

⅓ cup bread crumbs

½ cup half and half

1 egg, beaten

Salt and pepper, to taste

2 tablespoons butter

paTricia NeaL, 1926–2010

I N THE 1970S, PATRICIA NEAL WAS SIMPLY that patrician woman who sold Maxim on TV. But hawking instant coffee was only the tip of the ice cube. Neal won the Tony Award for Lillian Hellman's *Another Part of the Forest* in 1948. She played a housekeeper—and won an Oscar of her own to polish—opposite Paul Newman in the 1963 drama *Hud*. She had an affair with Gary Cooper when she was in her twenties and was married for decades to Roald Dahl, the guy who wrote *Charlie and the Chocolate Factory* and *James and the Giant Peach*. She was fascinating on stage and screen and even more impressive off.

Raised in Tennessee, Neal wanted to perform since she was ten and wrote a letter to Santa Claus asking for acting lessons. She got them at Northwestern University in Evanston, Illinois. (Go, Cats!) Later, braving New York, she found stage work and became one of Hellman's favorite performers by the time she was in her early twenties. When Hollywood called, Neal found roles in 1949's *The Fountainhead*—that was where Cooper came into the picture—the classic 1951 sci-fi thriller *The Day the Earth Stood Still*, Elia Kazan's 1957 drama *A Face in the Crowd* starring a very different Andy Griffith than we would see in Mayberry, and 1961's *Breakfast at Tiffany's*. Her stage triumphs during these years included *The Children's Hour* and *The Miracle Worker* on Broadway.

In 1965, while pregnant, Neal suffered brain aneurysms, lapsed into a coma, and nearly died. Three years later, though, she returned to the big screen in *The Subject Was Roses*, and was nominated for another Oscar. Her great TV moment as Olivia Walton in *The Homecoming* in 1971 earned her a Golden Globe Award, but she wasn't asked to continue in the role when the TV movie led to *The Waltons*. Producers felt that Neal might not be able to

a CHrisTmas HomecominG

161

handle the rigors of a weekly series. But she continued to act for almost forty more years.

Neal's life—punctuated with tremendous heartbreak—was chronicled in a 1981 TV movie, *The Patricia Neal Story*. Glenda Jackson played her. Dirk Bogarde was Dahl. I'm not sure, but I'm guessing that shilling instant coffee was not a big part of it. The recipe that follows, though, first appeared in a Maxim ad.

PATRICIA NEAL'S SUNSHINE PARFAIT

Prepare the instant pudding according to package directions. Divide half the pudding among 6 parfait glasses. Add a layer of orange sections to each and then the rest of the pudding. Garnish with additional orange sections. Right before serving, top each with a dollop of whipped cream or topping.

Serves 6

1 (3.4 ounce) box vanilla instant pudding

2 cups cold milk

2 oranges, sectioned

1 cup whipped cream or topping

POST MORTEM

If you're going to use instant pudding and Cool Whip, you might as well go totally period and use canned mandarin orange segments instead of fresh oranges. The early 1970s will come rushing back faster than you can say, "Goodnight, John-Boy!"

a DOZEN HOLIDAY PLATTERS

As long as there has been Christmas, there's been Christmas music. Okay, they may not have been singing "Away in a Manger" outside the actual manger, but since the 13th Century, tunesmiths have been writing holiday music in the vernacular. Thank God for that! Actually, it was St. Francis of Assisi who helped the trend along. Think of it: Without his patron saint, Francis Albert Sinatra may never have sung "Let It Snow! Let It Snow! Let It Snow!"

Seasonal religious hymns may be the most appropriate—a good "O Come, All Ye Faithful" can be downright stirring!—but it's the secular music, the novelty songs, and the truly weird holiday platters that get things going under the mistletoe. "Bring a Torch, Jeannette, Isabella" is never going to do for your evening what "Baby, It's Cold Outside" can. And "What Child Is This?" doesn't hold a candle to "All I Want for Christmas Is My Two Front Teeth" around the wassail bowl after you've had a few.

With that in mind, here are a dozen of my favorite Christmas hits, the dead celebrities who recorded them, and twelve delicious recipes to go with them. Think of each of these songs as the "Last Christmas," "All I Want for Christmas Is You," or even "Mr. Hankey the Christmas Poo" of their day. Spin them while you cook, or eat, or whatever, this and every holiday season.

eartha kitt, 1927–2008

"Santa Baby"

OTHER SINGERS FROM MADONNA TO MISS PIGGY to Macy Gray have tried over the years, but no one has ever begged Kris Kringle for more finery (or had a better chance of getting it all) than Eartha Kitt did when she recorded "Santa Baby" in 1953. The actress, chanteuse, and international sex kitten—an exotic creature whom Orson Welles once called "the most exciting woman in the world"—wrung every bit of gold-digging deliciousness out of the song and made it a novelty hit that endures today as the feline femme fatale's shining-est moment.

Kitt found success with other songs like "Monotonous," "I Want to Be Evil," and "C'est Si Bon"—not to mention her disco hits "Where Is My Man?" and "Cha Cha Heels"—and she appeared on Broadway in such shows as *New Faces of 1952, Timbuktu!* in 1978, and *The Wild Party* in 2000. But for many of us, Kitt is most famous for stepping into Julie Newmar's catsuit to play the second-best Catwoman that the Caped Crusader ever faced on the campy 1960s version of *Batman*. Kitt most memorably terrorized Seventh Avenue (and real-life fashion innovator Rudi Gernreich) on the 1967 "Catwoman's Dressed to Kill" episode.

In the mid-'70s, Kitt played a fashion designer herself in the very funky blaxsploitation film "Friday Foster," opposite Pam Grier. Late in her life, although still performing on stage, Kitt became an award-winning voice actor. Her work in such projects as *The Emperor's New Groove, My Life as a Teenage Robot*, and *The Emperor's New School* was, as they say, purr-fect.

In the ultimate typecasting, Kitt gave voice to a cartoon cat in the charming 2001 Rankin/Bass animated Christmas special *Santa, Baby!* Vanessa Williams sings lead on the title song, backed up by Kitt and Patti Labelle (playing a magical partridge), then near the end of the show Kitt sings a disco-fied version of "Santa Baby," with some rap thrown in.

No, it wasn't as good as the original, but what is? No Christmas hit will ever be as fierce as Eartha Kitt's timeless classic. In the kitchen, too, she could make kitty litter out of most others. What rabbit wouldn't want to get crocked with her?

POST MOrTeM

If the thought of cooking adorable Monsieur Lapin makes you hopping mad—it is so much harder to eat a cute animal, isn't it?—substitute a chicken. Neither is very flavorful on its own, so it's unlikely that your tasters will cry *fowl*.

eartha kitt's crocked rabbit with winter vegetables

Rinse the rabbit pieces and pat them dry. Place them in a shallow dish (or a ziplock bag). In a mixing bowl, combine the mustard, garlic, rosemary, and one tablespoon of the olive oil. Whisk in the vermouth. Drizzle this marinade over the rabbit and cover (or seal) the container. Let the rabbit marinate 12 to 36 hours, turning it occasionally.

Soak an unglazed 4-quart clay cooker in cold water for 15 minutes. Remove the rabbit from the marinade, reserving the liquid. Dredge the rabbit in the flour and, over medium heat, brown the pieces in the remaining olive oil in a large fry pan. Drain it on paper towels. Remove the clay cooker from the water. Arrange the vegetables on the bottom of it and toss to combine. Arrange the rabbit pieces on top and pour the marinade over it all. Cover it.

Put the clay cooker in a cold oven. Turn the oven to 425 degrees. Bake for 30 minutes. Remove the clay cooker from the oven. Toss the rabbit and the vegetables. Return it to the oven, and bake the dish 90 minutes more, tossing every half hour.

- 1 (3–4 pound) rabbit, cut into serving pieces
- 1½ tablespoons Dijon mustard
- 2 garlic cloves, thinly sliced
- 1¼ teaspoons crumbled dried rosemary
- 3 tablespoons olive oil
- ¼ cup dry vermouth
- 2 tablespoons flour
- 6–8 cups thinly sliced and cored green cabbage
- 2 large carrots, peeled and sliced
- ½ pound parsnips, peeled and sliced

Dean Martin, 1917–1995

"Baby, It's Cold Outside"

WHEN ANYONE ELSE SINGS "Baby, It's Cold Outside," it sounds like date rape. But when Dean Martin croons it, you know his gal is not only happy he's putting the moves on her, she's praying for a blizzard.

Martin had enough charm and sex appeal to seduce anyone, including generations of fans. Whether he was playing straight man to Jerry Lewis in the movies, singing "Everybody Loves Somebody" on the radio, or presiding over a celebrity roast on television, Martin played the role of the ultimate party boy better than anyone. Who else could say, "You're not drunk if you can lie on the floor without holding on," and make it seem like sober advice?

In more than fifty films—including *Bells Are Ringing, Rio Bravo, The Young Lions,* and *Airport*—Martin was a suave but funny leading man. I always liked him as Matt Helm, the James Bond–esque superspy he played in four films now classified as "martini movies." He had fans from *Cannonball Run,* too.

Martin's TV shows, which included *The Dean Martin Comedy Hour* and *The Dean Martin Celebrity Roasts,* were parties to which all of America was invited. They're starting to make their way onto DVD. And while his singing was always overshadowed by his proximity to Frank Sinatra, Martin's brilliant catalog of music will live on for generations. If you're thinking of throwing a Rat Pack–style Christmas party, well, Martin has an app(etizer) for that.

A Rat Pack Christmas with Martin, Davis, and Sinatra.

Dean Martin's Baked Potatoes with Caviar

6 small baking potatoes

½ cup sour cream

Onion salt, to taste

¼ cup caviar

Preheat the oven to 400 degrees. Scrub the unpeeled potatoes and then bake them until done. When they're just cool enough to handle, cut them in half, and scoop out enough of each potato to make 12 shells.

Whip the potato pulp with the sour cream and the onion salt. Spoon this mixture back into the potato shells. Top each one with a teaspoon of caviar and serve as an appetizer.

Maxene andrews, 1916–1995

● ● ● ● ● ●

"Mele alikimaka"

MAXENE ANDREWS WAS THE MIDDLE of three Andrews Sisters—a group so in sync they're even dying in order. Over their long career, which began with the hit "Bei Mir Bist Du Schoen," they sold more than 75 million records, appeared in numerous films, and even were a hit on Broadway in the early 1970s.

Nobody ever boogied or woogied (or even polkaed) better than they did in the '30s and '40s on such songs as "Hold Tight, Hold Tight," "Beat Me Daddy, Eight to the Bar," "Beer Barrel Polka," and, of course, "Boogie Woogie Bugle Boy." The girls had a thing for fruit trees, too, recording both "(I'll Be With You) In Apple Blossom Time" and "Don't Sit Under the Apple Tree."

Who knows why? It was a different time then.

Their contributions to Christmas music were considerable, too. Recording alternately with Bing Crosby and Guy Lombardo, their seasonal hits included "Jingle Bells" in 1943, "Winter Wonderland" and "Christmas Island" in 1946, "Santa Claus Is Comin' to Town" in 1947, and "Merry Christmas Polka" in 1950.

Their 1950 version of "Mele Kalikimaka" has been on my Christmas playlist since we threw a Hawaiian Christmas five or six years ago. (We used leis instead of garlands and all the ornaments were half-naked island girls.) While the song has been covered by everyone from Don Ho to The Puppini Sisters, no one has bested the original by our favorite trio. Only Bette Midler's version comes close to stealing the crown.

It would have been nice if Maxene had left behind a Hawaiian recipe, but alas, hers is for a Greek—*ish*—rice dish, which reflects half her heritage. Andrews was Norwegian on her mother's side. You *could* serve it in pineapples.

a Dozen Holiday Platters

171

The Andrews Sisters, stacked.

maxene andrews's greek-style rice pilaf

Heat a large saucepan over medium heat. Add the pine nuts and the noodles, crushing the noodles by hand as you add them. Toast the pine nuts and the crushed noodles, stirring all the while, until they begin to brown. Add the rice and stir for a minute. Add the margarine and stir until it melts. Slowly add the chicken stock. Stir. Cover and simmer for 20–25 minutes, or until all the water has been absorbed.

¼ cup pine nuts

½ cup fine egg noodles, uncooked

1 cup rice, uncooked

1 tablespoon margarine

2½ cups chicken stock

POST MORTEM

If you want to serve Maxine Andrews's Greek-Style Rice Pilaf as part of a vegetarian meal, substitute vegetable broth, store-bought or homemade, for the chicken broth. The recipe already calls for margarine instead of butter, so you're good to go.

"RUDOLPH THE RED-NOSED Reindeer"

WITHOUT GENE AUTRY, there would have been no "Rudolph the Red-Nosed Reindeer." Without Rudolph, there would have been no Christmas special about an elf who wants to be a dentist. And without that special and that elfish little tooth-puller there would be no Chapter 8 in this book. So let's just agree that we all owe Autry big time when it comes to Christmas.

The singing—and yodeling—cowboy didn't write "Rudolph"; that was Johnny Marks's creation. But it was Autry's biggest hit, selling 30 million copies over the years. And it was such a success in 1949 that the following year, he recorded another classic, "Frosty the Snowman." (See Chapter 8 again.) He also recorded "Peter Cottontail," but this book isn't about Easter.

So much a part of Christmas in America, these holiday standards capped a long, lucrative career for Autry. He appeared in nearly 100 movies—including 1935's *The Phantom Empire* and 1949's *The Big Sombrero*—and shot almost as many TV episodes of *The Gene Autry Show* between 1950 and 1955. Pat Buttram, who went on to play the conniving Mr. Haney on *Green Acres* in the '60s, was a frequent sidekick, appearing with Autry in more than forty films.

Born in Texas and raised in Oklahoma, where he worked as a ranch hand, Autry made it big in show business—for years, he was on the *Forbes* list of the richest Americans—but he took being a cowboy seriously. He was long involved with professional rodeo. And he helped establish the Museum of the American West in Los Angeles's Griffith Park. Autry is, interestingly enough, the only celebrity to have five stars on Hollywood's Walk of Fame—one in each category of performance. So put that in your ten-gallon hat and smoke it!

When it came to leaving behind a recipe, chili was a natural.

Gene Autry's Texas Chili

Serves 4-6

Brown the ground round, garlic, onion, and green pepper until tender in a large pan. Add all the remaining ingredients except the cheese and simmer for 1 hour over low heat. Top the chili with the cheese and stir just before serving.

1½ pounds lean ground round

1 clove garlic, chopped

1 medium onion, chopped

1 medium green pepper, chopped fine

1 package chili seasoning mix

Cayenne pepper sauce, to taste

1 (16 ounce) can kidney beans

1 (14½ ounce) can of diced tomatoes

1 cup grated Monterey Jack cheese

"THE CHRISTMAS SONG"

IF YOU KNOW HIM only as Natalie Cole's father—and posthumous duet partner—you don't know nearly enough about Nat "King" Cole. The man had twenty-eight gold records, charted such hits as "L-O-V-E," "Unforgettable," and his signature "Mona Lisa," wrote "Straighten Up and Fly Right" and had his own weekly variety program—featuring such guest stars as Frank Sinatra and Sammy Davis Jr.—at a time when sponsors wouldn't advertise on a show starring an African American.

Before he was crowned "King," Cole was playing church organ in Chicago and, with his brother, formed his own band in his early teens. Although he became a terrific jazz pianist, Cole's smooth baritone was his ticket to fame. Many first heard him with the King Cole Trio on radio programs in the 1930s and '40s. Throughout his career he straddled both jazz and pop, and when TV supplanted radio, he was a pioneer with 1957's *The Nat King Cole Show* on NBC. When no national advertisers could be found for the program, Cole remarked that "Madison Avenue is afraid of the dark." Paging *Mad Men*!

As for "The Christmas Song," it was written by the great Mel Torme, one of the many Jews who've written enduring Christmas songs, and Cole recorded it four times, beginning in 1946. An early 1960s version is the one we know and love best. Although he died young, his music lives on. Songs he made famous are heard on the soundtracks for films and series as varied as *Raging Bull*, *Watchmen*, *The Sopranos*, and *Six Feet Under*. And every Christmas, chestnuts roast on an open fire.

They'd be a nice accompaniment to Cole's ham loaf.

Cole in your stocking.

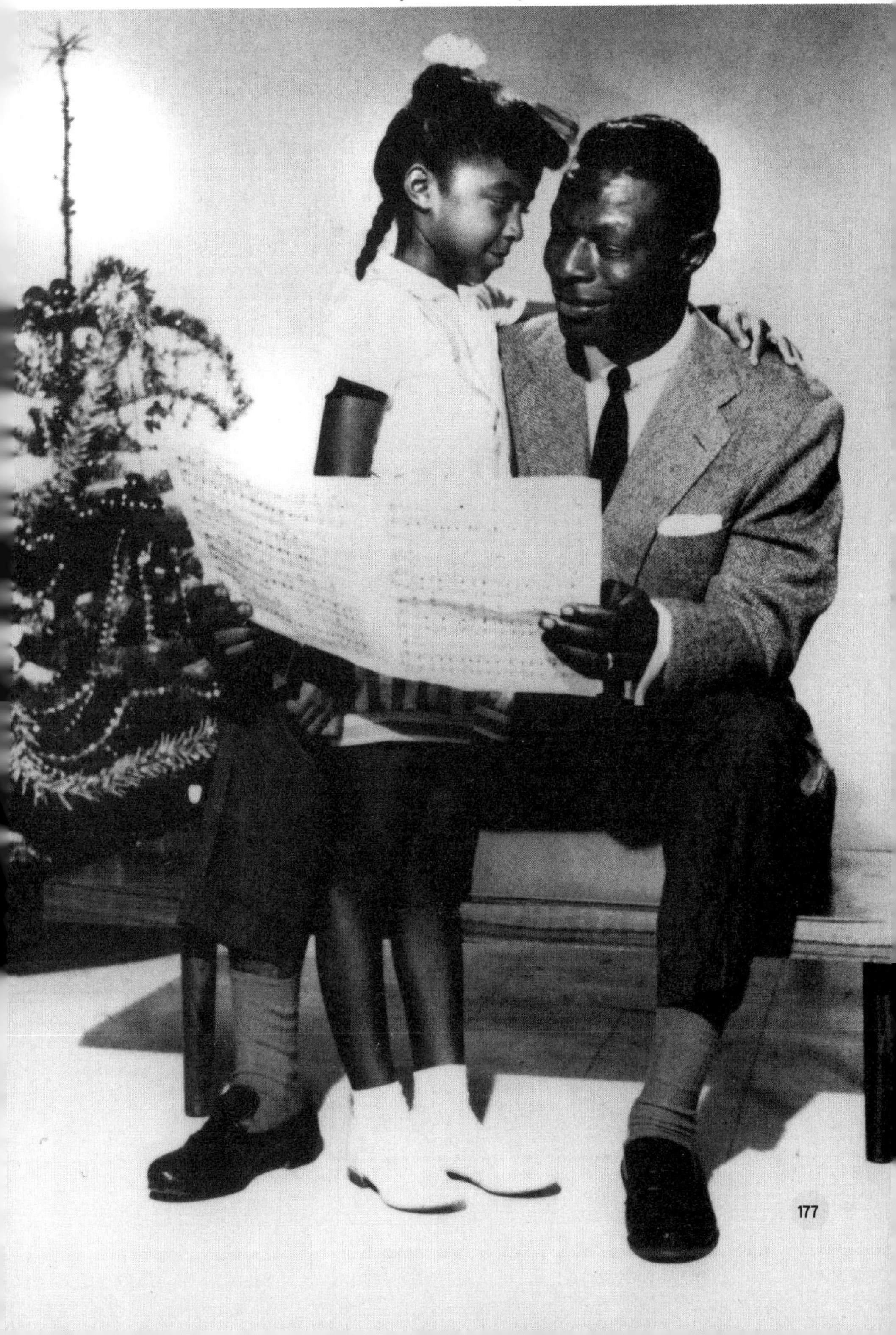

NaT "KinG" cOLe'S BaKeD Ham LOaF

Preheat oven to 275 degrees. Grind the ham using a food processor or a food grinder. Mix the ground ham well with the ground pork, eggs, milk, and cracker or corn flake crumbs. Add the Worcestershire sauce, mustard, and the salt and pepper. Form the meat mixture into a loaf and place it into a baking pan. If desired, thickly cover the loaf with the brown sugar before baking.

Bake the ham loaf for 3 hours. Remove it from the oven, wait 20 minutes, slice it, and serve.

Serves 8

2 pounds cooked ham

1 pound fresh ground pork

2 eggs, beaten

¼ cup milk

1 cup crushed crackers or corn flakes

1 tablespoon prepared mustard

1 tablespoon Worcestershire sauce

Salt and pepper, to taste

¾ cup brown sugar (optional)

"Blue Christmas"

E WAS THE KING—A SINGER, ACTOR, AND HEARTTHROB whose swivel hips were a lethal weapon capable of slaying young girls by the millions. Although he died young, Elvis Presley managed to record ninety charted albums, log eighteen No. 1 singles, sell more than a billion records, and win three Grammys. And holiday gloom never sounded better than Elvis singing "Blue Christmas."

Beginning with his first single, "Heartbreak Hotel," which topped the charts in 1956, Presley became a superstar of the burgeoning musical genre called rock 'n' roll. The native of Tupelo, Mississippi brought what had been African American music to the white masses with songs like "Blue Suede Shoes," "Hound Dog," and "Don't Be Cruel." His thirty-one movies (*Viva Las Vegas, Jailhouse Rock,* and *King Creole* among them) capitalized on his sexiness. Honestly, you haven't seen steamy until you've seen him soaking wet in an Army uniform in *Blue Hawaii.*

Elvis's career was so big in the 1950s and '60s that his induction into the armed services and his marriage to a teenaged Priscilla were front-page news. Although his career suffered a bit during the British Invasion, Presley scored major victories with two televised concerts. His 1968 comeback special (the one with all the black leather) and 1973's *Aloha from Hawaii* (the one with the spangled white jumpsuits) were TV events. More than a billion people (my family included) watched the latter, broadcast via satellite around the planet.

Presley's death four years after that lei-laden TV special stunned the world, but it also launched a legion of Elvis impersonators and one of the most lucrative posthumous careers in history. Since his death, he's had a huge dance hit with a remixed version of "A Little Less Conversation," "toured" in 1997 via film, and spawned a lavish Cirque du Soleil show in Las Vegas. Even his 1993 postage stamp was a record-breaker, selling more than any other commemorative in history!

What's most amazing is that even decades after his death, Presley is still with us. Elvis never really left the building after all. Here he is in the kitchen.

eLVIS PresLeY'S HUSH PUPPIeS

Combine the corn meal, onion, flour, baking powder, baking soda, and the salt in a large bowl. Beat the egg and buttermilk together. Add the liquid ingredients all at once to the dry ingredients. Mix until well blended.

Heat the oil in a large saucepan or deep fryer to 375 degrees. Carefully drop the batter by the tablespoonful into the hot oil in small batches. Do not crowd. Fry the hush puppies for several minutes, turning often, until well browned on all sides. Remove from the oil with a slotted spoon and drain on paper towels. Serve hot.

2 cups corn meal

⅓ cup chopped onion

1 tablespoon flour

1 teaspoon baking powder

1 teaspoon baking soda

1 teaspoon salt

1 egg, well-beaten

1½ cups buttermilk

Oil for deep frying

POST MorTem

The only thing better than fresh, hot hush puppies is fresh, hot hush puppies served with maple butter. To make ¾ cup of this irresistible condiment, whip together ½ cup softened butter with ¼ cup real maple syrup using an electric mixer. It's heaven on warm muffins or toast, too!

PEGGY Lee, 1920–2002

"CHrISTMaS Carousel"

WHEN PEGGY LEE PENNED AND SANG "Christmas Carousel"—the title track to a 1960 holiday album that mixed her original compositions with classics like "White Christmas"—she added to a brilliant legacy of song that includes such classics as "Fever," "Is That All There Is?," "I'm a Woman," and the title song to *Johnny Guitar*, a fabulous film that finally saw the light of DVD in 2012.

The sophisticated chanteuse in the platinum bob was a three-time Grammy winner and, as an actress, an Oscar nominee for her supporting role in the 1955 film "Pete Kelly's Blues." Lee was also the voice of the dog Peg in the Disney animated classic *Lady and the Tramp*. I saw her cabaret act late in her life. The woman sat in a swivel chair, didn't get up once, and was pure genius.

Lee's six-decade-long career began on radio in her native North Dakota. She was playing a club in Chicago when bandleader Benny Goodman noticed her and signed her up for a two-year stint beginning in 1941. She had a hit the following year with the song "Somebody Else Is Taking My Place," but her 1943 million-seller "Why Don't You Do Right?" made her a star. A string of hits followed in the '50s, and her 1956 album *Black Coffee* is considered one of the all-time greats. I have a soft spot for 1960's kitschy *Latin ala Lee!* myself.

Although she was famously left out of the memorial montage at the Oscars in 2002, Lee does have a rose named in her honor, and as someone who was often called "*Miss* Peggy Lee" despite having been married and divorced four times, she is said to have been the inspiration for Miss Piggy. Miss Piggy *did* sing "W-O-P-I-G" that time on *The Muppet Show*. Lee's Holiday Halibut Casserole recipe lives on, too. Is that heartburn or fever? You decide, baby.

PEGGY LEE'S HOLIDAY HALIBUT CASSEROLE

Serves 4-6

2 pounds halibut

1¼ teaspoon salt

¼ teaspoon white pepper

¼ pound butter

2 tablespoons flour

1 cup milk

1 (10½ ounce) can condensed tomato soup

¾ cup grated cheddar cheese

½ pound mushrooms, sliced and sautéed

1 cup frozen green peas, thawed

2 tablespoons A-1 sauce

Dash cayenne pepper

Season the fish with the salt and pepper. Melt 2 tablespoons butter in a broiling pan. Place the fish in the pan and broil it 8 minutes per side, or until the fish flakes easily when tested with a fork. Skin and debone the fish and cut it into cubes.

Melt 4 tablespoons butter in a saucepan. Blend in the flour, then the milk, and then the soup. Stir the sauce until it begins to boil. Add ½ cup of the cheese and stir until it melts. Add the sautéed mushrooms, peas, A-1 sauce, cayenne pepper, and finally the fish. Turn the mixture into a buttered casserole dish. Sprinkle with the remaining cheese and dot with the remaining butter. Bake the casserole for 20 minutes or until it has browned and is bubbling hot.

karen carpenter, 1950–1983

"merry christmas darling"

SHE HAD ONE OF THE GREATEST, MOST distinctive voices of the twentieth century and nothing—not even her tragic death as a result of anorexia—could diminish that. Karen Carpenter was a tiny person with enormous talent.

Her voice, showcased best on the 1971 track "Superstar," was heavenly and heartbreaking, which is what made her 1978 recording of "Merry Christmas Darling" so special. A modern holiday classic, it's both wistful and beautiful—like Karen herself—and one of the finest songs that she and her brother Richard ever performed together.

A squeaky-clean duo from Downey, California, the Carpenters gave the world such soft-rock classics as "(They Long to Be) Close to You," "Rainy Days and Mondays," and "For All We Know" and became one of the best-selling acts of the 1970s. Their songs were an easy-listening alternative to the hard rock of the day, and twelve of their singles became Top Ten chart hits. Take that, headbangers!

One of their greatest gifts was their 1978 album *A Christmas Portrait*. A landmark recording, it contains not only "Merry Christmas Darling" but also a lilting version of "Christmas Waltz" and a rip-your-guts-out rendition of "Have Yourself a Merry Little Christmas" that is surpassed only by Judy Garland's original.

When *The Dead Celebrity Cookbook* came out in 2011, some interviewers asked me whether it was tasteless to include a recipe from a celebrity with an eating disorder. Perhaps. But the way I look at it, *any* reason to mention Karen Carpenter and keep her memory alive is a good one. To reiterate what

Karen Carpenter, her muff, and her brother.

I said then, don't be friends with anyone who doesn't like the Carpenters. Certainly don't waste a Christmas card on them. And don't share even one bite of your Peach Mabel!

karen carpenter's peach mabel

Crush the vanilla wafers in batches in a food processor (or in a plastic bag using a rolling pin) and mix them with the butter. Spread the mixture on the bottom of an 8 × 11 baking dish, saving some crumbs to sprinkle on top.

Combine the extracts, the salt, and the sugar in the food processor. Blend well. Add the egg and blend. In a small bowl, mix the gelatin with the water and stir to dissolve. Add this to the egg-sugar mixture and blend well.

In another bowl, whip the heavy cream until stiff and then fold it into the other ingredients. Fold in the drained and diced peaches. Sprinkle with the reserved cookie crumbs and refrigerate for several hours before serving.

1 box vanilla wafers

4 tablespoons butter, softened

1 teaspoon vanilla extract

1 teaspoon almond extract

½ teaspoon salt

¾ cup sugar

1 egg

1 envelope unflavored gelatin

¼ cup cold water

1 pint heavy cream

2 cups canned peaches, drained and diced

"THe TWeLve DaYs OF CHristmas"

H E'D WORKED WITH ARTIE SHAW and Mitch Miller, and arranged music for such luminaries as Rosemary Clooney and Johnny Mathis. But in 1957 when he started recording under his own name, Ray Conniff struck gold. The light, breezy sound of the Ray Conniff Singers—formed two years later—is the essence of lounge music.

Whether the 1966 hit "Somewhere My Love" (as "Lara's Theme" from *Dr. Zhivago* is better known) or 1967's "Pearly Shells" off *Ray Conniff's Hawaiian Album,* his music sounds good in an elevator and even better if you're sitting on a leopard-print banquette. Call it schmaltzy, but I prefer the word Conniff himself used to title a 1974 album: "The Happy Sound of Ray Conniff."

As for his contributions to holiday cheer, Conniff's 1959 album "Christmas with Conniff" was a huge seller. But my favorite of his many Christmas tracks is the Ray Conniff Singers' rendition of "The Twelve Days of Christmas" from the 1962 follow-up "We Wish You a Merry Christmas." Less pinkie ring than the Sinatra Family's Jersey version and considerably shorter than Dinah Shore's on the *Pee-wee's Playhouse Christmas Special* (see Chapter 10), it is what holiday shopping in the '60s sounded like. Heaven at E. J. Korvettes'.

Conniff saw twenty-eight of his albums hit the Top 40 charts between 1957 and 1968, when rock supplanted the kind of pop he was making. He kept recording until the last few years of his life, though, and lived long enough to see his music become hip. Neo-lounge lizards embraced him—as those who'd bought 70 million of his albums over the years had—as part of the so-called "Cocktail Revolution." Conniff was not only popular again, turning up on soundtracks to *There's Something About Mary* and *Mad Men*, he had become cool.

His easy-to-make wine cake will knock your mittens off.

RAY CONNIFF'S WINE CAKE

Preheat the oven to 350 degrees. In a large bowl, combine all of the ingredients and beat for 5 minutes with an electric mixer at medium speed. Pour the batter into a greased and floured 10-inch tube or Bundt pan.

Bake the cake for 45 minutes or until the cake springs back when touched. Cool the cake in the pan for 5 minutes, then turn it out on a rack, and cool completely. Before serving, sprinkle the cake with confectioners' sugar.

Serves 10

1 (18.25 ounce) package yellow cake mix

1 (3.4 ounce) package vanilla instant pudding mix

4 eggs

¾ cup oil

¾ cup sherry

1 teaspoon nutmeg

Confectioners' sugar

MARLENE DIETRICH, 1901–1992

"THE LITTLE DRUMMER BOY"

AS AN ACTRESS IN THE 1930S, she set Hollywood on its ear with films like *Shanghai Express* and *Blonde Venus*. Marlene Dietrich was one of the most glamorous, most exotic creatures ever captured on film, bending gender lines before RuPaul's *parents* were born. So what if she had a speech impediment that made her sound like Baba Wawa. Dietrich was Dietrich, and that means fabulous.

Born in what is now part of Berlin, Dietrich started her showbiz career as a chorus girl in that divinely decadent German city. She did some stage acting and dabbled in film before landing her breakthrough role as Lola-Lola in Josef von Sternberg's *The Blue Angel*. In the film, she introduced her signature song "Falling in Love Again." Dietrich went on to make such films as *The Scarlet Empress, The Devil Is a Woman, Desire,* and *I Loved a Soldier*. In 1939, having become an American citizen, Dietrich performed in *Destry Rides Again,* opposite James Stewart, and premiered the song "The Boys in the Back Room."

From the 1950s to the 1970s, Dietrich toured with a cabaret act. Burt Bacharach (yes, *that* Burt Bacharach) was her musical director, and did his best with her limited vocal abilities. She may not have been a great singer, but she could act a song splendidly. Her 1964 version of "The Little Drummer Boy" has a lot more gravitas than the Harry Simeone Chorale's rendition. Dietrich, the film director and critic Peter Bogdanovich once observed, "transcends her material. She lends an air of the aristocrat, yet she never patronizes."

a DOZEN HOLIDAY PLATTERS

189

Dietrich made a couple of notable appearances later in her career, including Orson Welles's amazing 1958 thriller *Touch of Evil* and Stanley Kramer's 1961 drama *Judgment at Nuremberg*. Her final film appearance was opposite David Bowie in 1978's *Just a Gigolo*. But the 1984 documentary *Marlene*, directed by actor Maximilian Schell, in which only the octogenarian Dietrich's voice was used, is a better coda. See it if you can. Here's Dietrich's way with dessert.

Marlene Dietrich's zabaglione

Beat the egg yolks until creamy and then stir in the Marsala. Pour the mixture into a double boiler that has been placed over slowly simmering water and beat it with an electric mixer until it almost doubles in volume. Serve the zabaglione warm in stemmed glasses.

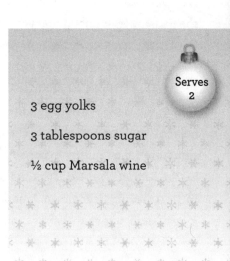

Serves 2

3 egg yolks

3 tablespoons sugar

½ cup Marsala wine

"ALL I WANT FOR CHRISTMAS IS MY TWO FRONT TEETH"

NOT TO BE CONFUSED WITH SPIKE JONZE, THE GUY who made Beastie Boys videos, was married to Sofia Coppola, and directed *Where the Wild Things Are*, Spike Jones was a bandleader who used cowbells, toilet plungers, and all kinds of junk as instruments to create musical mischief. Jones's backup musicians, known as the City Slickers, weren't called "the band who plays for fun" for nothing. They specialized in what Jones called "musical depreciation," and no genre was safe.

Jones had a big hit in 1942 with "Der Fuehrer's Face," a war song that gave Adolf Hitler the Bronx cheer. With cartoonish silliness, Jones turned "Cocktails for Two" into a riot by adding honking horns, cigarette coughs, and a chorus of hiccups; he gargled his way through the "William Tell Overture" and remade the "Hawaiian War Chant" into a truly loony tune. What the man did to opera was even stranger. Leoncavallo would have died if he heard Jones's "Pal-Yat-Chee."

In time for the 1948 holidays, Jones scored a No. 1 hit with his best-remembered tune, "All I Want for Christmas Is My Two Front Teeth," which expressed the singular wish of one dentally challenged boy. (Santa, please, the little brat just wants to wish you Merry Christmas without whistling!) It made him a favorite of a new generation of warped music-lovers, including Dr. Demento, Weird Al Yankovic, and Frank Zappa.

Jones wrote and recorded almost until his death, satirizing Elvis Presley, the rise of folk-pop, and more. You've got to love a guy who would release an album called *Dinner Music for People Who Aren't Very Hungry*. Of course, when you *are* hungry, there is Jones's holiday cookie recipe. His Molasses Jumbles turn out almost as deliciously cracked as he was.

SPIKE JONES'S MOLASSES JUMBLES

Preheat the oven to 375 degrees. With a wooden spoon, beat the shortening until it's fluffy. Gradually incorporate the sugar. Add the molasses and stir well. Sift the dry ingredients together and add them to the mixture alternately with the water. Stir until combined. Drop the batter by heaping tablespoons onto greased cookie sheets. Bake them for 8 to 10 minutes.

Serves 8

5 tablespoons vegetable shortening

½ cup brown sugar, firmly packed

1 cup molasses

1 tablespoon baking soda

¼ teaspoon salt

3½ cups all-purpose flour

½ cup cold water

"Happy Xmas (war is over)"

SO MAYBE IT'S NOT "IMAGINE," but John Lennon's song "Happy Xmas (War Is Over)," written with his wife, Yoko Ono, and released in 1971, has become a Christmas standard and will always embody the utopian visions that Lennon and Ono championed. The lyrics—"War is over, if you want it"—came almost wholesale from the billboards the couple put up as part of their 1969 campaign against the Vietnam War. Sadly, they continue to be timely.

Lennon, as a singer/songwriter and the most beloved Beatle of all, was responsible (along with Paul McCartney) for some of the greatest songs of the second half of the twentieth century. From "All You Need Is Love" to "Yellow Submarine," Beatles music has been the soundtrack of our lives since the 1960s. The band has sold upwards of a billion records—more than any other group—and one need only listen to "The White Album" or *Rubber Soul* or *Revolver* to know why.

As a solo artist, Lennon penned and recorded his seminal hit "Imagine" the same year as "Happy Xmas (War Is Over)." That song has been called one of the greatest singles of all time. Along with Ono—a controversial but important artist in her own right—Lennon wasn't just a performer, but also an important activist who asked the world to "give peace a chance." Together, they were dedicated to love and brotherhood. Ono and Lennon really believed that the world could be a better, more nurturing place if we all wanted it to be.

Such abundant good will made Lennon's 1980 assassination outside the Dakota, the New York City apartment building in which he lived, a devastating moment. We all remember where we were when we heard the awful news that one of the all-time greats had been taken from us. Every Christmas we think of Lennon, and the enduring sentiment of "Happy Xmas (War Is Over)." Others, from Neil Diamond to Maroon 5, have recorded cover versions of the song over the years, but none has improved upon the original. Here's Lennon's original recipe for hot cocoa. It may be the least of what he left us, but it'll warm you on a cold December day.

JOHN LENNON'S HOT COCOA

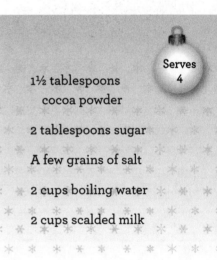

Mix the cocoa, sugar, and salt in a saucepan. Dilute with ½ cup of the boiling water and stir to make a smooth paste. Add the remaining water and boil for 1 minute. Add this to the scalded milk and beat the mixture with an electric mixer for 2 minutes on medium speed. Pour the cocoa into mugs and serve.

Serves 4

1½ tablespoons cocoa powder

2 tablespoons sugar

A few grains of salt

2 cups boiling water

2 cups scalded milk

13

JUST a LITTLe CHristmas NOW

As Christmas movies go, they're horror shows. But there's something wonderful about them, too, which is why a certain group of fellas— boys, you know who you are—are crazy about *Mame* and *Mommie Dearest*. These films are camp classics that deserve an annual viewing sometime between Halloween and the lighting of the Rockefeller Center tree. They're nightmares before Christmas.

In the 1974 movie version of *Mame*, Lucille Ball rasps her way through the delightful Jerry Herman musicalization of *Auntie Mame* about Beekman Place's most free-thinking glamour girl. It doesn't matter that when Lucy opens her mouth to sing, she makes Harvey Fierstein sound like Katy Perry. She's still lovable in *Mame*, even at sixty-two. She's no Rosalind Russell, who starred in the original 1958 nonmusical version *Auntie Mame*, but who is?

Of course, if Lucy hadn't stolen the lead in the movie musical from Angela Lansbury, who originated the role on Broadway in 1966, we would probably like *Mame* in an entirely different way. As it is, you sit and wonder what it might have been had Lansbury re-created her Tony-winning performance, as her costar Bea Arthur (see Chapter 9) does as boozy bestie Vera Charles. It might have been a glorious movie musical, instead of an absolute scream.

Lansbury, they say, is still unhappy that her take on the role wasn't preserved for posterity. She and Arthur did re-create their bravura duet "Bosom Buddies" on the 1987 Tony Awards telecast. You can watch it on YouTube or as part of the 2004 DVD compilation *Broadway's Lost Treasures II*. Both actresses were past sixty, but they still shimmied (and shimmered) as fabulously as ever.

The number that makes the movie *Mame* a holiday panic, of course, is "We Need a Little Christmas."

Gauze for Alarm: Ball in *Mame*.

In the story, Mame Dennis's net worth goes south along with everyone else's in the stock market crash of October 1929. But rather than be glum about it, she decides that she and her youthful ward Patrick Dennis (Kirby Furlong) should "haul out the holly" and decorate his nanny Agnes Gooch (Jane Connell). The old virgin looks quite festive in tinsel and lights, as it turns out.

Even though "it hasn't snowed a single flurry," the gang—including man-servant Ito (George Chiang)—exchanges presents. To bring the song home, Mame puts on a Santa mask and struts around the living room. That's when it gets scary. Let's just say it is not Lucy's best look. As film critic Dennis Dermody has said, "When she dons a transparent mask and croaks, 'We need a little Christmas,' she's more frightening than *Friday the 13th*'s Jason."

The scene is not as frightening, however, as the way Christmas is portrayed in 1981's over-the-top film biography *Mommie Dearest*, starring the inimitable Faye Dunaway as Joan Crawford.

First, Joan has sex in the shower with Uncle Greg (Steve Forrest), one of the many "uncles" for whom daughter Christina (Mara Hobel) has to fix drinks, and then she runs off to hang out with nuns and distribute Christmas presents to needy children. "Being here with you and the children at Christmas is one of the things I most look forward to," Joan says. Well, sure, Joan, after you've banged some hunk in the shower of your Brentwood mansion, it's probably a nice change of pace to hang out with poor people and brides of Christ.

But the brilliance of *Mommie Dearest*, as it relates to Christmas, comes a little later in the juxtaposition of two of the film's most famous scenes. First, a kabuki-faced Joan goes nuts when she finds a wire hanger in little Christina's closet and tosses Old Dutch cleanser everywhere.

The next thing you know, it's Christmas Eve and the Crawfords are America's most perfect family as they conduct a radio broadcast from their beautiful home. "Mother's fans send us so many things," Christina says. Of course, the kids aren't allowed to keep most of them. The real Joan Crawford actually says in the radio broadcast (you've got to YouTube it!) that she uses

Christmas as a teaching moment. "I always see to it that they give up something they really love, otherwise they don't really learn the value of giving."

How frigged up is that?

On the December 16, 1978, edition of NBC's *Saturday Night Live*, Gilda Radner (whose Dutch Apple Cake recipe is included in *The Dead Celebrity Cookbook*) and Jane Curtin did a hilarious spoof of the Crawfords at Christmastime. The episode, hosted by Elliott Gould, is on the Season Four box set but not included on the show's Christmas compilation DVD. Since those days of edgy late-night TV comedy, drag queens from coast to coast have been putting together Crawford-themed Christmas shows, although I'm not convinced that any are as funny as Gilda and Jane.

Whether you go see one of these productions around the holidays or simply stay home some night, cook up Lucy and Joan's recipes, and watch a *Mame/Mommie Dearest* double feature—if you dare!—I have one suggestion: Don you now your gay apparel.

LUCILLE BALL, 1911–1989

WHETHER WRAPPING CHOCOLATES, stomping grapes, smuggling home an enormous cheese by dressing it as a baby, or tossing dinner rolls through a pass-through kitchen window, no one has ever been better at side-splitting shtick than Lucille Ball. She was—and still is—the reigning queen of physical comedy.

On *I Love Lucy* in the 1950s, *The Lucy Show* in the '60s, and *Here's Lucy*, which ran into the mid-'70s, Ball made a hilarious mess of everything she touched. Thanks to her, calamity always became comedy.

It's also why we forgive her for *Mame*.

Before her television triumphs, Ball was a leggy "Goldwyn Girl" with a movie career dating back to the early 1930s. She was in the 1937 comedy drama *Stage Door* with Katharine Hepburn and Ginger Rogers; the 1938 Marx Brothers picture *Room Service*; Dorothy Arzner's 1940 musical *Dance, Girl, Dance*; the 1943 fantasy *Du Barry Was a Lady* with Red Skelton (see Chapter 8); and the 1950 comedy Western *Fancy Pants* with Bob Hope.

Ball appeared in a number of pictures with her greatest partner, husband Desi Arnaz, but none compared to their TV work. Not even 1953's *The Long, Long Trailer*. But how could it? *I Love Lucy* is as perfect a sitcom as there has ever been. After Ball and Arnaz split in 1960, she filled her limited time off from making weekly television by filming numerous specials and such features as the 1968 blended-family comedy *Yours, Mine and Ours* with Henry Fonda.

Ball quite vocally claimed she didn't care about food other than as fuel to get through her day. But she left behind numerous recipes. A half dozen of them appear in *The Dead Celebrity Cookbook*. This one brings the total up to seven. It's as nutty as Lucy Ricardo ever was, and just exotic enough to serve at one of Mame's rollicking soirees.

Serves
8

LUCILLE BALL'S BRAZIL NUT STUFFING

2 onions, chopped

½ cup butter

2 cups chopped Brazil nuts

3 cups crumbled stale corn bread

Salt and pepper, to taste

Sage, to taste

Water, milk, or chicken stock (optional)

In a large sauté pan, cook the onions in the butter over medium heat until tender but not brown. Add the nuts and the corn bread crumbs and stir for 2 minutes. Season the stuffing with salt, pepper, and sage. If the mixture seems too dry, moisten it with a bit of water, milk, or chicken stock.

Stuff a 10-pound turkey, or, to cook the dressing separately, place it in a greased casserole and bake for 1 hour.

POST MORTEM

Toasting the Brazil nuts before you use them will give this stuffing added flavor. To do so, place the nuts in a single layer on a cookie sheet and bake in a 325-degree oven for about seven minutes. If the nuts look slightly brown and they smell good, they're done. Let the nuts cool completely before chopping them.

Joan Crawford, 1905–1977

I KNOW. TECHNICALLY, JOAN CRAWFORD WASN'T IN *Mommie Dearest*. But Faye Dunaway embodied Crawford so thoroughly that these days many of us can't immediately tell the difference between a picture of the actress who shone so brightly in *Network* and *Bonnie and Clyde*—that would be Faye—and an image of the shoulder-padded icon of *Queen Bee* and *Johnny Guitar*. It's very confusing, because both are such damned good actresses.

The real Joan Crawford was responsible for some of the most indelible performances ever put on film—the temptress Sadie Thompson in *Rain*, the ultimate mistress Crystal Allen in *The Women*, the manipulative domestic diva in *Harriet Craig*—the list goes on and on.

Her role as the self-sacrificing restaurateur in *Mildred Pierce* won her the Academy Award for Best Actress, but she was great in so many others—*Daisy Kenyon, Sudden Fear, The Best of Everything, Whatever Happened to Baby Jane?*, and even *Torch Song* in which she appeared (no joke!) in black face. Even her really bad films—*Strait-Jacket* and *Trog*—are fun. She's pretty terrific in the pilot for Rod Serling's *Night Gallery* TV series, too.

Crawford was an obsessive-compulsive personality, which means she was a terrific housekeeper. She didn't just clean, she was mad at the dirt! And as the drag artiste (and sometime Crawford impersonator) Lypsinka says in the DVD extras for the "Hollywood Royalty" edition of *Mommie Dearest*, Crawford "was almost obsessed with Christmas." Like everything else in her tightly controlled life, she wanted to make it picture-perfect.

In the book upon which *Mommie Dearest* is based, Christina Crawford says Christmas was only fun while the cameras were rolling. Then it was back to the glamour gulag for her and her adopted siblings. The elder Crawford offers life lessons in her legendary book, *My Way of Life*. You might want to get your hands on a copy to read while her angel food cake is in the oven.

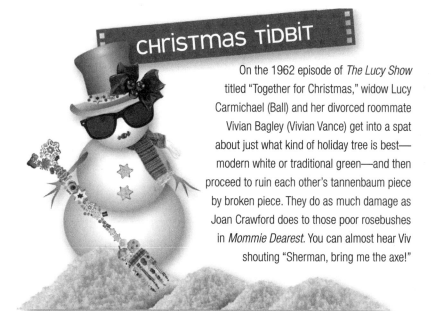

CHRISTMAS TiDBiT

On the 1962 episode of *The Lucy Show* titled "Together for Christmas," widow Lucy Carmichael (Ball) and her divorced roommate Vivian Bagley (Vivian Vance) get into a spat about just what kind of holiday tree is best— modern white or traditional green—and then proceed to ruin each other's tannenbaum piece by broken piece. They do as much damage as Joan Crawford does to those poor rosebushes in *Mommie Dearest*. You can almost hear Viv shouting "Sherman, bring me the axe!"

Joan crawford's angel food cake

Preheat the oven to 350 degrees.
Sift the cake flour and ⅞ cup sugar
together three times.

In a large bowl, beat the egg whites,
cream of tartar, vanilla, almond extract,
and salt until foamy. Add the remaining sugar, 2 tablespoons at a time, and
beat until stiff peaks form. Gradually
sift the flour mixture over the beaten
egg whites and fold it in, just until the
flour disappears.

Spoon the batter into an ungreased
10-inch tube pan, and gently cut
through the batter with a knife to
spread it evenly. Bake for 1 hour. Let
it cool for 10 minutes and then invert
onto a rack to cool completely.

1 cup cake flour

⅞ cup, plus ¾ cup sugar

Whites from 12 large eggs

½ tablespoon cream of tartar

½ tablespoon vanilla

¼ teaspoon almond extract

¼ teaspoon salt

14

Mr. & Mr. New year's eve

I t was late on December 31, 1974. I had just turned twelve and should definitely have been in bed already, and my family was in a quandary.

Should we tune our eighteen-inch black-and-white Zenith television
to Guy Lombardo's annual New Year's Eve special as we always did—which,
if you'd asked me at the time, was just a ballroom full of fuddy duddies in
their finest duds close-dancing to (yawn) Big Band music—or should we
watch something new and infinitely hipper called *New Year's Rockin' Eve*
with Dick Clark?

Well, you know how I voted—Dick, all the way!—and you know who was
overruled: me. If you had Italian American parents who were born in 1919
and 1922, as mine were, you were going with old, faithful Lombardo.

We *always* watched Lombardo, and, yes, he seemed antique *even then*.
That was one of the reasons Clark started his own New Year's Eve celebration in the first place. As mad as I was that first year of Clark's alternative to
canapés and curmudgeons, I'm happy today that we watched Guy Lombardo
and his Royal Canadians play to what looked like a sea of insurance sales-
men and their wives.

That night, I was witnessing the end of an era—a hokey one, maybe, but a
major era nonetheless. Lombardo's performances weren't consciously retro
or ironic—there was no wink in what he did—they just were what they had
always been since 1929. He enthusiastically played songs that he'd been performing since my parents were kids. His "Auld Lang Syne" was their "Auld
Lang Syne," and in his last few years, it was my "Auld Lang Syne," too.

For the record, my mother *hated* that song. But I see it now as a bridge
to an earlier era and a way to connect to who my parents had been before I
arrived in 1962. Those couples waltzing past the camera were like my parents in the '50s, when my mother wore a veiled hat on her head and a stone
marten around her neck as she sipped a Sidecar in a leopard-skin booth at

the Café Zanzibar, and my father wore pinstriped suits and drove a Desoto. Those Guy Lombardo broadcasts were a window into a posh world that I hoped to experience as an adult.

Dick Clark's *New Year's Rockin' Eve* is still with us, of course, even though Dick is no longer. Ryan Seacrest, competent and likeably bland, has inherited the mantel. It's not quite the appointment viewing it once was. These days, if we're home on New Year's Eve, we just tune in to see the ball drop in Times Square and then turn the set off again. This year, though, I'm going to make Dick Clark's Spicy Turkey Meatloaf and Guy Lombardo's Lobster Lombardo seafood-and-noodle casserole. Both are reminders of New Year's Eve long—and not so long—ago, and tasty ways to usher in the future.

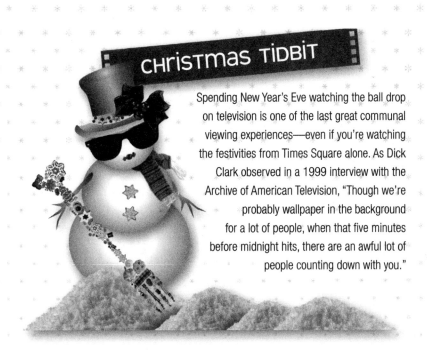

CHRISTMAS TIDBIT

Spending New Year's Eve watching the ball drop on television is one of the last great communal viewing experiences—even if you're watching the festivities from Times Square alone. As Dick Clark observed in a 1999 interview with the Archive of American Television, "Though we're probably wallpaper in the background for a lot of people, when that five minutes before midnight hits, there are an awful lot of people counting down with you."

DICK CLARK, 1929–2012

● ● ● ● ● ● ● ● ● ●

AS THE HOST OF *American Bandstand* and the man who brought rock 'n' roll into living rooms every day, he became known as "America's oldest teenager." Forever youthful in appearance and demeanor even after a 2004 stroke, Dick Clark was an eternal presence on television from the 1950s until nearly the end of his life. His easygoing manner and just-handsome-enough visage made him supremely likeable, and his sharp business acumen made him a force to be reckoned with in the entertainment industry.

Clark started out as a radio DJ, became the host of TV's *Bandstand* in Philadelphia in 1956, and then took the show to Los Angeles eight years later. At that point, there was no stopping this real-life Corny Collins. The show became a cultural landmark, and Clark became a star. Once *Bandstand* began incorporating live performances into its record hop format, Clark became a hit-maker. He is credited with making rock palatable to parents. Truly, everybody who was anybody during his years at the helm of *American Bandstand* got their earliest TV exposure on Clark's show.

In addition to his *Bandstand* hosting duties, he went on to emcee the various denominations of *Pyramid* game shows; he created and produced the American Music Awards; and in the mid-'70s launched a yearly alternative to traditional New Year's programming. Loud and hip as it alternated pretaped performances with a countdown live from Times Square, Clark's yearly *Rockin' Eve* specials were the antithesis of Guy Lombardo's staid broadcast.

Over the years, Clark was honored with Emmy Awards and a Peabody, and was inducted into numerous halls of fame. His work in front of the camera—hosting such series as *TV's Bloopers & Practical Jokes* and a male version of *The View* called *The Other Half*, or acting on *Perry Mason* or *The Fresh*

Clark was *Rockin'* 'til the end.

Prince of Bel-Air—is done. But Clark did so much work behind the scenes that his presence will continue to be felt in showbiz for years to come. Certainly, no New Year's Eve will go by without a nod to the now eternal teenager.

Here's his recipe for Spicy Turkey Meatloaf.

DICK CLARK'S SPICY TURKEY MEATLOAF

Sauté the onions and add them to the ground turkey along with the beaten egg and the bread crumbs. Stir well, but don't overmix. Combine all of the spices and add to the turkey. Mix well and shape the meat into a loaf. Place the turkey meatloaf into a roasting pan and refrigerate for 1 hour.

Preheat oven to 350 degrees and bake the meatloaf covered with aluminum foil for 45 minutes. Remove the foil and bake the meatloaf an additional 15 minutes.

Serves 4

¾ cup chopped onions

1½ pounds ground turkey

1 egg, lightly beaten

2 tablespoons dry bread crumbs

¼ cup chopped fresh basil (or 1 tablespoon dried)

¼ cup chopped fresh parsley (or 1 tablespoon dried)

2 cloves garlic, minced

½ teaspoon dried thyme leaves

½ teaspoon ground ginger

½ teaspoon crushed red pepper flakes

Salt and pepper, to taste

GUY LOMBARDO, 1902–1977

BANDLEADER GUY LOMBARDO NEVER HAD the rock 'n' roll street cred that Dick Clark did, but then he was from a different era. For the pre-rock generation, the leader of the Royal Canadians was Mr. New Year's Eve for nearly half a century.

A Canadian American of Italian heritage and a serious musician from his preteen years onward, Lombardo began the annual task of ushering in the New Year in 1929 on the radio. When he and his red-jacketed orchestra made the jump to television in 1956, America was watching and stayed with Lombardo for 20 years. Even after Clark began attracting younger viewers like me, Lombardo fans like my parents were loyal.

His annual broadcasts, first from New York's Roosevelt Hotel and later from the Waldorf Astoria, seemed like the height of chic, particularly during the *Mad Men* era. To watch couples in their finery fox-trotting past the camera was a hoot. Very *Muppet Show* ballroom, actually.

On many of the other 364 nights of the year, Lombardo busied himself performing. He appeared on numerous variety shows over the years—even the subversive hit *Laugh-In* in the late '60s—and did guest shots as himself on such series as *Route 66, Ellery Queen,* and *I've Got a Secret.* He always said his band created "the sweetest music this side of heaven." Now that Lombardo is on *that* side of heaven—we hope!—we're left with some enduring recordings and this recipe for a fancy seafood-and-noodle casserole he called "Lobster Lombardo." You'll have to decide if it's the tastiest dish this side of heaven.

Lombardo without his Canadians.

Serves 6

GUY LOMBARDO'S LOBSTER LOMBARDO

Preheat the oven to 400 degrees. Cook the spinach noodles according to package directions. Drain them and place them in the bottom of a buttered 2-quart casserole dish.

Melt 4 tablespoons of the butter in a saucepan over medium heat. Stir in the cream and heat it until hot but not boiling, stirring all the while. Cool the butter-cream mixture for 5 minutes, and then stir in the salt, pepper, sherry, Romano cheese, and beaten egg yolks. Cook it over low heat, stirring constantly, until the sauce is reduced by about a quarter. Add lobster meat to the sauce, mix it well, and pour it over the noodles in the casserole.

Top the casserole with the bread crumbs and the Parmesan cheese and dot it with the remaining tablespoon of butter. Bake for 20 minutes or until the crumbs begin to brown.

1 (8 ounce) package spinach noodles

5 tablespoons butter

1 cup light cream

2 egg yolks, beaten

1 teaspoon salt

A pinch of white pepper

½ cup sherry

½ cup grated Romano cheese

2 cups cooked lobster meat

2 tablespoons bread crumbs

3 tablespoons grated Parmesan cheese

a New Year's eve menu

My mother always maintained that it was good luck to eat pork on New Year's Eve—pigs supposedly symbolize progress, wealth, and prosperity. This menu is built around a stuffed crown roast. You may have to make your own luck, but the dish's festive richness will help you ring in a new year with a boffo dinner that's both chic and scrumptious.

starters
Edgar Bergen's Swedish Meatballs

Greer Garson's Guacamole

George Brent's Saratoga Potatoes

pasta
Lionel Barrymore's Fettuccine Alfredo

entrée
Jack Albertson's Stuffed Crown Roast of Pork

accompaniments
Alec Guinness's Baked Stuffed Peaches

Jimmy Durante's German Cole Slaw

desserts
Joan Crawford's Angel Food Cake with

Charles M. Schulz's Favorite Seven-Minute Frosting

one For THE ROaD

No matter how beautiful—or how artificial—your Christmas tree is, the day comes when you have to take it down. When I was growing up, we always waited until the Epiphany, which is twelve days after Christmas and commemorates the day the Three Wise Men finally showed up at the manger. It seemed like they got there so much sooner on *The Little Drummer Boy*, didn't it?

As an adult, we celebrate Christmas at our weekend house, which means the tree sometimes stays up a little longer. One year, it was up until Easter. It's pathetic because it's true. Even after all those extra months, I hate to see the ornaments get wrapped and boxed, and that big fake tree go back into its cardboard coffin for another year. Okay, seven months, but you know what I mean. Like that silly Wizzard song, I wish it could be Christmas every day.

The way to take the sting out of tree untrimming day—or at least a way to eat the pain away—is to make a batch of homemade cookies to enjoy between trips up the pull-down stairs to the attic. Norman Rockwell, an artist whose illustrations have shaped our notions of a traditional Christmas, left behind a recipe for his favorite oatmeal cookies. Dunked into a cold glass of milk and chased by a couple of aspirin, your taste buds will be happy and your back won't hurt nearly as much on the drive back home to the city apartment that night.

Norman ROCKWELL, 1894–1978

HIS COVERS FOR THE *Saturday Evening Post, Boys' Life*, and other magazines illustrated visions of American decency for more than four decades, and no one rendered "homespun" life with more sophistication. Norman Rockwell's paintings and drawings, whether of a family gathered around a festive turkey dinner, a sturdy Boy Scout setting sail, or three scrambling skinny dippers caught in the act, manage to steer clear of the cloying, even at their folksiest. The so-called "Painter of Light," Thomas Kinkade—God rest his soul—couldn't hold a candle to him.

Rockwell's holiday illustrations—many of which are collected in the 1977 volume *Norman Rockwell's Christmas Book*, which was updated in 2009—truly capture the spirit and wonder of December 25. The paintings are funny and likeable, and no matter how cynical you are, you can't help but want to live in them, or at least spend the holidays there. I know I would.

Surprisingly for someone whose visions seemed so rural, Rockwell was born in New York City. He knew he wanted to be an artist at 14, and was being published in national magazines before he was out of his teens. His tenure at the *Post* began when he was in his early twenties. He produced more than 300 covers for that magazine before going on to make paintings for *Look*. It was the 1960s, and Rockwell's eye turned toward pressing social issues of the day, like racism.

Although some critics dismissed him as kitsch during his lifetime, the tide turned at the end of the twentieth century. As a critic for the *New Yorker* wrote in 1999, "Rockwell is terrific. It's become too tedious to pretend he isn't." If a critic won't convince you, perhaps this will: His original paintings sell for upwards of $15 million. That's a lot of oatmeal cookies.

Norman Rockwell's oatmeal cookies

Preheat the oven to 400 degrees. Mix the butter with the brown and white sugars until well combined. Stir in the vanilla. Beat the water and eggs together and add them to the butter mixture. Sift salt, flour, and baking powder together and mix it in. Next, stir in the uncooked oatmeal, and then add the nuts. Stir just until combined.

Drop heaping teaspoons of the batter onto an ungreased baking sheet. Bake for 8 to 10 minutes.

¼ pound butter, softened

1 cup light brown sugar

½ cup sugar

1 teaspoon vanilla

¼ cup water

2 eggs

1 teaspoon salt

1 cup flour

½ teaspoon baking powder

1 cup uncooked oatmeal

1 cup chopped walnuts

POST MORTEM

Various versions of Norman Rockwell's recipe for oatmeal cookies exist, including one that suggests underbaking the cookies and then broiling them for a few moments to crisp them up. If you decide to go that route, be careful not to burn them or they'll end up at the curb with the Christmas tree.

acknowLeDGments

ESIDES THE DEPARTED STARS THEMSELVES, there are so many people to thank.

First, thanks to those who shared celebrity recipes from their own collections, particularly Greg Sobieraj and John Briggs, whose recipe-stuffed card of Christmas 2010 helped make *The Dead Celebrity Cookbook* such fun; Justin Berns, who uncovered William Frawley's recipe for Mulligan Stew; Simon Doonan, who generously bestowed upon me his copy of *Nobs and Nosh;* and Susan Mulcahy, who passed along Marlene Dietrich's Zabaglione recipe and who has been an angel to me over the years in more ways than I can count.

Thanks to those intrepid gourmands who helped test recipes for *The Dead Celebrity Cookbook*, especially Erica Berger, Frank Carabineris, and Sally Starin. They're three of my dearest dearests, and they all know their way around a kitchen even better than I do.

Thanks to Paige Greytok and her fiancé, Doug Conn, who said, as he was buying *The Dead Celebrity Cookbook,* "You should do a *Dead Celebrity* Christmas cookbook next." One question, Doug: Now what?

To those who helped me get the word out about *The Dead Celebrity Cookbook* by generously opening up their kitchens (and guest rooms) to me, especially Carr D'Angelo and Susan Avallone, James Sie and Doug Wood, Marc Wolf, and retroactively, Tom Jacobson and Ramone Munoz.

Huge thanks to Kim Weiss. A better book publicist does not exist. Trust me.

To my literary agent, Laura Dail, who held my hand for as long as I asked her to and who let go just at the right time.

Thanks to my Sirius XM colleagues Doria Biddle and Greg Sahakian, who made it possible for me to do a daily radio show and still meet something close to my book deadline. Much appreciation to all the listeners of *The Frank DeCaro Show*, too, who helped brainstorm ideas for this book, and to my desk-mate Keith Price for saying, "That turkey needs a toe tag on it." Big thanks to our hard-working interns, too! They do an awful lot for an awful little.

To my editor, Allison Janse, who never once said, "Where the hell is the manuscript?!"

To my husband, Jim Colucci, who not only copyedits the bulk of my work, but also helps keep me on the right track in any creative endeavor. The man has the patience of a saint and tremendous integrity, and I adore him. If I could get him to eat Chinese food on New Year's Eve, he'd be perfect.

And finally to Gabby—and darling Herman before her—for taking long naps with me when I really should have been writing. May visions of Milk-Bones dance in your head on Christmas and every day.

© Photo by Erica Berger

FRANK DECARO is heard each weekday morning on his own live national call-in program, *The Frank DeCaro Show,* on Sirius XM Satellite Radio. He is best known for his years as the movie critic on *The Daily Show with Jon Stewart,* and his stint on the game show *I've Got a Secret.* In South America, he is "Mr. Happy Chop." (Don't ask.)

DeCaro also co-created the 2010 YouTube sensation "Betty White Lines," a rap tribute to the *Golden Girls* star that was featured on the *Today* show, *Showbiz Tonight,* and dozens of blogs and got more than 100,000 hits in its first week online.

A graduate of Northwestern University's Medill School of Journalism, DeCaro has written for myriad publications including *Martha Stewart Living, Newsweek, Entertainment Weekly, Vogue* and *TV Guide.* In addition to *The Dead Celebrity Cookbook* series, he is the author of the groundbreaking memoir *A Boy Named Phyllis,* which *Vanity Fair* called "hilarious" and *The Advocate* credited as opening the door for David Sedaris and "the gay American humorist as everyman." His follow-up work, a coffee-table biography called *Unmistakably Mackie: The Fashion and Fantasy of Bob Mackie,* is now a highly coveted collectible.

DeCaro lives in New York City and New Jersey with his writer husband Jim Colucci and their mischievous Boston terrier Gabby. Visit the author at deadcelebritycookbook.com, "like" him on Facebook, and follow him @frankdecaroshow on Twitter.

INDEX